THE FOREIGN EXCHANGES

CT/W/£10·00

THE FOREIGN EXCHANGES

Theory, Modelling and Policy

MICHAEL BEENSTOCK

Foreword by

JOHN WILLIAMSON

First published 1978 by
THE MACMILLAN PRESS LTD
London and Basingstoke
Associated companies in Delhi
Dublin Hong Kong Johannesburg Lagos
Melbourne New York Singapore Tokyo

Printed in Hong Kong

British Library Cataloguing in Publication Data

Beenstock, Michael
   The foreign exchanges
   1. Foreign exchange
   I. Title
   332.4'5   HG3821

   ISBN 0–333–22369–1

Contents

Contents

Foreword

British monetarism is not what made British economics famous. Nevertheless, there is one characteristic feature of the contributions of such home-grown monetarists as Britain has produced in the past two decades that in my view does them enormous credit and could profitably be emulated by their peers in other countries, and that is their practice of incorporating their ideas within structural models rather than resorting to black boxes or reduced forms. This was conspicuously true of the two main groups of academic monetarists—David Laidler and Michael Parkin and their colleagues in the Manchester Inflation Workshop, and the backbone of the International Monetary Research Programme at LSE; it has also been generally true of Sam Brittan, Peter Jay, and the other financial journalists who have propagated monetarism at the semi-popular level in Britain, and of the authors of Greenwell's Monthly Bulletin who brought monetarism to the City of London; and, as this book helps make clear, it is emphatically true of the former backroom monetarists of H. M. Treasury, Michael Beenstock and Patrick Minford. This willingness to embody ideas within structural models is courageous, inasmuch as it involves deliberately refraining from playing some of the tricks of 'How to Create a Revolution in Economic Thought (and further one's career in the process)', as dissected in one of Harry Johnson's most brilliant essays ('Revolution and Counter-Revolution in Economics', *Encounter*, April 1971). It is also immensely helpful in elevating controversy from polemic to rational discussion.

Michael Beenstock's book falls squarely in this laudable tradition of British monetarism. He offers us a structural macroeconomic model of an open economy which incorporates the standard building blocks of Keynesian theory, and demonstrates that in the long run this model exhibits all the characteristic monetarist properties. The conclusion that a short-run Keynesian model (provided it is augmented by virtually any species of Phillips curve and a correct treatment of money supply accounting) leads to long-run monetarist conclusions is not new, but it is important, and it has seldom been spelled out more clearly or forcefully. It is a conclusion which offers the basis for an honourable truce between those who regard themselves as monetarists and those who, like myself, still react more sympathetically to the adjective 'Keynesian'. Both can endorse the synthesis represented by the sort of structural model constructed and examined in the first three chapters of this book. The ability to agree on so much is a fruit of the rational approach that I have praised as a characteristic of the British monetarists.

The first reason that I believe this book deserves attention is, therefore, that it offers a careful and comprehensive account of the manner in which valid and important contributions from both monetarist and Keynesian traditions can be integrated into a framework that should be acceptable to both schools, and which, moreover, has the advantage of being a good description of reality. I would also point to a second reason why any serious economist needs to become thoroughly familiar with a model of this general class. The reason is the seemingly paradoxical one that for most purposes the model is too complex to actually use. One therefore generally adopts a simpler model to handle specific problems—an IS/LM model, or a quantity theory model, or a model with no forward market. This type of simplification can be immensely helpful when carefully used, but it can also be extremely dangerous when improperly used. (A full employment quantity theory model, for example, is extremely useful for analysing the genesis of hyper-inflation, but worthless for analysing the problem of how to stop an ongoing moderate inflation.) And one can judge which features are crucial in generating what sort of behaviour, and which aspects can legitimately be ignored as merely complicating without fundamentally altering the results (i.e., when simplification is legitimate), only by developing a feel for the general model.

Endorsement of the structural model does not, of course, dispose of the monetarist – Keynesian controversy. What it does do is suggest that the crucial question for deciding on a range of issues that have typically divided monetarists and Keynesians is not the basic structure of the system, but rather the question 'how long is the short run?' Acceptance of the accelerationist theory of inflation, for example, pretty well commits one to treating the natural rate of unemployment as a target level of unemployment. (I say 'pretty well' because this statement really needs two not-unimportant glosses: first, that one might want to set the target unemployment rate above, or in principle below, the natural rate for a while so as to squeeze excessive inflation, or in principle disinflation, out of the system; and second, that one might want to try to reduce the natural rate itself, whether by incomes policies or microeconomic labour market policies—however one chooses to distinguish between those two.) But there remains a question as to whether it is sensible to use demand management policies to seek to hasten the convergence of the economy to this target unemployment rate. If the Keynesian short run lasts five or ten years, there appears ample scope for such policies; if the monetarist long run arrives in two years or less, the only sensible policy is the monetarist steady course.

But this is not the end of the story. The newest element to be injected into the debate by the monetarists, which is repeatedly emphasised by

Michael Beenstock, concerns the rationality of expectations. If expectations are rational, in the sense that the participants in private markets use all available information to make the best possible forecast of the future, then (barring asymmetries in information, etc.) there is no reason to suppose that the authorities will be better able to forecast the future than the private market, and every reason to suppose that, if the authorities try to manipulate the market to achieve their own objectives, the market will be able to respond to undo the policies being pursued. It is further argued that the effect of rational expectations is in many cases to telescope what would otherwise be a lengthy adjustment process, and that where adjustments still require time this is because, for example, certain stock adjustments inherently require time and there is nothing that policy can hope to do to improve matters. Not only does the monetarist long run usually arrive quickly, but if it doesn't this is for good reasons that have to be respected.

Whether rational expectations necessarily and always have all these implications is probably the most exciting and important issue being discussed by economic theorists at the present time. Personally, I tend to be impressed by the fact that we observe phenomena, such as prolonged depressions and strikes, that would not occur in a world of thorough-going rational expectations, and hence to doubt whether we shall end up with as extreme a picture of the futility of activist government policies as that urged by Michael Beenstock. But the jury is still out on this one.

The jury—i.e. the economics profession as a whole—should certainly be interested in the empirical evidence presented in this book suggesting that the formation of exchange rate expectations is consistent with the hypothesis of rationality. Indeed, the empirical estimates presented in the second half of the book provide the final reason that makes me happy to commend this book to fellow economists. The outstanding finding in this connection is that of extraordinarily low interest sensitivity of short-term international capital movements. (Low as these figures are, it should not be thought that they can be ruled out on account of incompatibility with the well-known fact that vast sums cross the exchanges when a step devaluation is expected. Take, for example, the estimate that a 1 per cent rise in UK interest rates induces a short-term inflow of £64.5m. (p. 184). Applying this figure to an expected depreciation of, say, 14.5 per cent expected in two weeks' time, i.e. to an interest rate of 3083 per cent at an annual rate, gives a predicted capital outflow of almost £200 billions!)

It is possible that these estimates are the result of faulty econometrics—perhaps, for example, a consequence of the assumption that interest rates are exogenous when in fact they are determined simultaneously with capital flows (see Kouri and Porter (1974).) But (see Chapter 7) this is by no means the only study that has found international capital mobility to be markedly less than many theorists customarily assume. The implications of such limited capital mobility are, of course, far reaching. Under fixed exchange rates, it implies that the monetary approach to the balance of payments is valid only in the long run, and that the 'traditional theory'—income effects, elasticities, etc.—retains an important place in explaining not just the composition of the balance of payments but also the overall currency flow in the short run. Under flexible exchange rates, it implies that the full-blooded asset market theories of exchange rate determination that have swept the board with scarcely a murmur of dissent over the past two years need important modifications—in fact, that they need modifying toward the alternative flow specification that as it happens I offered at the same conference where the asset market theories were first introduced (*Scandinavian Journal of Economics*, 1976 (2)). And, although for the past two years I have rather regretted my failure to spot the bandwagon, on reflecting on these results, I wonder whether my regrets were misplaced. Moreover, the stock version of the asset market theory needs implausibly large swings in monetary policy, or in the market's estimates of future monetary policies, in order to account for the volatile (20 per cent plus) swings in exchange rates that we have in fact observed under floating, whereas this is not true of the flow version of the theory.

I have said enough to indicate why I believe this book will be found worthwhile, if not particularly easy, reading to many economists, and why even those who disagree with the author in many respects can recognise the importance of the subjects discussed. It is a pleasure to see yet another reflection of the fact that Macmillan have not joined that growing band of publishers who have apparently decided to confine their activities to the hamburger of the publishing trade, the textbook, but are still prepared to publish the research results of scholars who have not yet become widely known.

John Williamson
Rio de Janeiro
September 1977

Preface

This book has largely been written on the basis of my experiences and work as an economic adviser in the Overseas Finance Section at H. M. Treasury between January 1973 and July 1976. It is also a development on my Ph.D. dissertation 'Forward Exchange Markets, International Capital Movements and the Balance of Payments', which was submitted to the University of London in 1976. In many respects this was a very exciting if at times depressing period in the economic history of the U.K. in particular and the world in general. A number of currencies were making their first tentative steps at floating, inflation among the industrial countries became a serious threat for the first time in the post-Keynesian era, the OPEC oil price hikes of 1973–74 raised a number of major questions about the structure of the international economy, some countries are managing to run balance of payments deficits whose size would have been inconceivable only a few years ago, and the world economy has experienced its deepest recession for over a generation.

As well as this dramatic back-cloth, this study reflects innumerable discussions with many colleagues. In particular I would like to thank Patrick Minford, John Hutton and Marcus Miller for their constant advice, criticism and encouragement over the years. Bill Allen, who was my opposite number at the Bank of England, did a great deal to keep me on my toes, and in the later stages Steven Bell proved to be an invaluable colleague and sounding-board for many of the ideas developed. In the final analysis, of course, responsibility for all views and errors of omission and commission rests entirely with myself. In particular none of the views should necessarily be attributed to the organisations with which I have been professionally associated.

My final thanks are to John Williamson for his Foreword, and to the World Bank, which enabled me to complete the final drafts.

MICHAEL BEENSTOCK

Washington, D.C.
June 1977

Introduction and Preview

Main Issues

This study is largely concerned with the theoretical and empirical determinants of the capital account in the balance of payments. To this end, it ranges over several key interrelated areas. First and foremost among these is the substitutability of financial assets of different currency denominations. If an investor substitutes a financial asset from country A for a financial asset from country B a transaction in foreign exchange will be involved and the capital account of country B will be improved. Whereas transactions on the current account of the balance of payments concern the substitution of goods from different currency areas, transactions on the capital account concern the substitution of financial assets from different currency areas.

The essential difference between the substitution of financial assets and claims within a currency area and the substitution of financial assets and claims from different currency areas is that the latter involves an additional element of risk in the form of the uncertainty associated with future exchange rate developments. Transactions on the capital account inevitably involve an assessment of the expected change in the exchange rate over the holding period on the part of the investor. Therefore, the second key issue that will be investigated in the study is exchange rate uncertainty and the role and determination of expectations.

In the past there may have been some tendency on the part of empirical researchers to regard unobservables such as expectations as yet another hurdle for the already hard-pressed econometric model-builder to overcome; and consequently, largely for the sake of completeness, to represent expectations by one proxy or another that would seem to have some plausible explanation. This has been as true in the case of research into the behaviour of the foreign exchange markets as in other areas of economic research. The main assumptions have tended to be that expectations are either formed adaptively along the lines first discussed by Nerlove [1957] or they are extrapolations of previous developments as in the tradition of Modigliani and Sutch [1966]. More recently, however, it has been increasingly realised, e.g. Sargent and Wallace [1975], Barro [1976], Modigliani [1977], that the way in which expectations are formed is crucial to the policy assessments for which economic models are often used, in which case the treatment of expectations comes to the forefront of empirical investigation in contrast to the back-seat position that has been typical in the past. Despite the fact that the Rational Expectations Hypothesis first invented by Muth [1961] has been known for a number of years, since approximately 1973 there has been something of a Rational Expectations 'revolution' which has preoccupied a large number of economists on both sides of the argument. Accordingly, in this study particular attention is paid to the treatment of exchange rate expectations both theoretically and empirically, and particular emphasis is laid on the Rational Expectations Hypothesis.

The third key area of research is the role of the foward exchange markets in the determination of capital flows. It will be argued that an analysis of the forward market and an empirical assessment of the responses in the forward market are essential for an adequate assessment of policy with respect to the capital account of the balance of payments. If, for example, the authorities raise domestic interest rates relative to overseas interest rates, it is necessary to know not only the elasticity of substitution between international financial assets, but also, to the extent that international investments are covered forward, the supply of forward cover from other participants in the foreign exchange markets. In other words, the forward market is an integral aspect of the analysis of short-term capital flows. This view, which originated with Keynes [1923] and was revived among others by Tsiang [1959] and Sohmen [1966] more recently, is analysed in further detail in the present study.

The capital account is made up of short-term and long-term flows. To a greater or lesser extent the distinction here must be arbitrary and is analogous to the distinction between short-term bills and long-term bonds in the context of the term structure of interest rates, i.e. bonds are less liquid and long-term borrowing may serve as a 'preferred habitat' for the long-term investor. Ultimately the distinction between long and short-term flows is an empirical issue in so far as long-term capital moveents are associated with long-term interest rates and short-term capital with short-term interest rates. No capital flows model would be complete therefore without an analysis of long as well as short-term capital flows. Accordingly, a parallel issue to those already mentioned is the theoretical and empirical investigation of long-term as well as short-term capital movements. The policy maker in particular is interested in ascertaining the sensitivity of the balance of payments to long-term as well as to short-term interest rate policy; and in the past it would seem, e.g. Hodjera [1971], Hutton [1977], that short-term capital movements are often regarded as the main policy vehicle on the capital account through which the authorities might seek to influence the balance of payments. In contrast, this study indicates that the capital account may be as sensitive to interest rate policy at the long end as it is at the short end.

Wider Issues

While we are largely concerned with the theoretical and empirical determinants of the capital account in the balance of payments, an important related aspect of the study is a theoretical investigation into the long-term determinants of the balance of payments as a whole when the exchange rate is fixed and the long-term determinants of the exchange rate itself when the exchange rate is assumed to float. Indeed this part of the study lends itself to a number of fundamental policy conclusions which may not be widely appreciated by some policy practitioners. In addition, this investigation goes a considerable way in reconciling many of the deductions usually associated with the 'monetarists' with the arguments of those who contend that the policy prescriptions of the 'monetarists' are too simplistic and that the complicated structure of the macro-economy does not lend itself to any simple and clear-cut panaceas regarding employment, inflation and the balance of payments. In particular it is shown that large-scale structural econometric models, when fully specified, logically relate in the long run to the major 'monetarist' deductions that inflation is a monetary phenomenon, e.g. Friedman [1968], and that when the exchange rate is fixed the balance of payments is determined by the processes of monetary creation, as discussed by Johnson [1972].

Alternatively, the investigation sets out the conditions which would have to be fulfilled for the 'monetarists' and their opponents to disagree, given the marco-economic framework that is proposed. This investigation would seem to be particularly worthwhile, since it is rarely the case that econometric models are ever completed and the economic system upon which they are based logically closed. Moreover, the relationship between some econometricians and their models, especially the large multi-sector multi-equation models, is at times reminiscent of the relationship between Dr Frankenstein and his monster, with the monster often inexplicably behaving in ways that were never intended. As with the monster's few loose wires, models with loose ends and poor specifications may swiftly lead to nonsensical policy recommendations. It is therefore important to be aware of the logical properties implicit in the model to be estimated so that the plausibility of its estimated version can be assessed.

To this end a macro-economic model is proposed wherein the balance of payments measures the foreign exchange transactions of a country in terms of its current and capital account components. In this way, the balance of payments may usefully be regarded as the excess demand function for spot exchange. If the current or capital accounts of the balance of payments strengthens, the excess demand for domestic currency relative to overseas currency will increase. If the exchange rate is fixed, the excess demand for the currency must be balanced by an equal and opposite supply of domestic currency made available by the authorities. It is through this mechanism that the foreign exchange reserves increase. If the authorities do not balance the spot market, the market will tend to clear via, among other factors, the price of foreign exchange. It is through this mechanism that the exchange rate floats.

The balance of payments identity, or the market for spot exchange, is the meeting place for several other markets which determine its constituent parts. First, the current account may be broken down into imports and exports. Exportables will tend to compete with import substitutes and non-traded output from the point of view of the allocation of domestic resources. In the essentially neo-classical world with which we intend to deal, the principle of allocation in the longer run would tend to be that of relative profitability. Similarly, on the demand side, the domestic demand for importables, import substitutes, exportables and non-traded output would relate, among other things, to income and relative prices. Among these other factors would be monetary factors so that the pressure of aggregate demand would be related to interest rates, real balances etc. Actual exports would also depend upon the overseas demand for exports.

If the current account largely interacts with these real markets, the capital account interacts with financial markets and of course the forward exchange markets. We have already noted that the capital account concerns the international substitution of various financial assets which in their turn interact with the domestic money markets in the various countries.

Any excess demand or supply in any one of these markets will tend to spill over into neighbouring markets both directly and indirectly. For example, an increase in the supply of import substitutes would tend to lower the price of import substitutes in relative terms and strengthen the current account through the reduction of imports. If the exchange rate is freely determined, this would tend to drive up the exchange rate, thereby reducing the overseas demand for exportables and reducing profit margins on exportables. The change in the spot rate for a given forward rate would alter the cost of forward cover, which in turn would generate capital movements in the balance of payments.

Likewise, domestic monetary developments such as an expansion in the money supply would tend to repercuss on to other markets. In the first instance, a monetary expansion would tend to lower interest rates and raise the demand for real output as a whole. If the monetary expansion was the result of an increase in government expenditure, this expenditure would add directly to aggregate demand. Lower interest rates would tend to generate short and long-term capital movements, thereby affecting both spot and forward rates. The spot market would also tend to be affected by a weaker current account as higher aggregate demand raised prices, reduced export competitiveness and raised import demand.

The balance of payments, when viewed as the market for spot exchange, therefore influences and is in turn influenced by other aggregate markets that make up the macro-economy. In practice, it is unlikely that these markets will adjust instantaneously, so that what we are likely to have is a dynamic general equilibrium system where the balance of payments or the market for spot exchange reflects equilibrium tendencies and adjustment processes in other markets, especially the markets for money and traded goods.

Alternative Approaches to the Balance of Payments

For want of a better turn of phrase the balance of payments analysis that has just been summarised may be called the 'structural approach', since the balance of payments is determined through the entire structure of the economy. This approach is essentially eclectic since it draws exclusively on existing intellectual developments. The novelty lies in the integration of these theoretical building blocks into a single structure and the exploration of the analytical consequences. By explicitly incorporating traded and non-traded goods the 'structural approach' takes under its wing the generalised elasticities theory of the current account. By being flexible enough to include income-expenditure mechanisms as part of the dynamic structure of individual markets, the 'structural approach' takes into consideration the Keynesian foreign trade multiplier theory.

Apart from Keynes's earlier work in the *Tract on Monetary Reform*, to which reference has already been made, it was not until the development of the 'absorption approach' to the balance of payments as, for example, described by Johnson [1958] that financial and monetary factors were rediscovered to be important in the determination of the balance of payments i.e. before the revival of Hume's price-specie flow mechanism under the 'monetary approach'. The 'absorption approach', while relating to the current account, may be extended to the balance of payments as a whole. If expenditures are greater than receipts the balance of payments would be in deficit regardless of whether this excess of absorption was of a real or financial origin, i.e. whether or not it originated on the current or the capital account.

There is therefore an affinity between the absorption approach where net excess absorption may be considered as the combined public and private sector financial deficits and the so-called neo-Cambridge theory of the balance of payments which relates the balance of payments to the public sector financial deficit on the assumption that the private sector surplus is broadly constant over time. In other words, if the public sector financial deficit increases *ex post*, this must lead to over-absorption, or to an overseas sector financial surplus given the constancy of the private sector surplus.

The neo-Cambridge theory is a recent development in British academic circles and is mainly associated with the Cambridge economists, Godley, Cripps, Nield and Kaldor. The theoretical model has been described in Cripps and Godley [1976] and the empirical model has been covered in Fetherstone [1976]. An early critique of the approach may be found in Kahn and Posner [1974]. The main conclusions of the approach may be summarised as follows:

(*a*) Because the private sector financial surplus is assumed *ex hypothesi* to be broadly constant over time, variations in the balance of payments must be broadly equal and opposite to variations in the public sector financial deficit via conventional accounting identities.
(*b*) Since exports are assumed to depend on the exchange rate and the balance of payments is through (*a*) independent of the exchange rate, the main role of the exchange rate is to determine the level of domestic economic activity and the volume of employment.

The intention here is not to describe and evaluate in detail the various balance of payments theories that have evolved, but merely to relate the 'structural approach' to which the work in this study adheres to its antecedents and contemporaries. While an authoritative review of all these theories and their empirical value has yet to appear, a brief survey may be found in Frenkel and Johnson [1976, Chapter 1]. Nevertheless, it should be pointed out that whereas the 'structural approach' generalises the previous theories so far discussed, the assumptions, if not the conclusions, of the neo-Cambridge theory would conflict with the specification of the 'structural approach'. The conclusions of the neo-Cambridge theory largely follow from the assumption that the marginal propensity to save is zero and that the only source of leakage from the domestic economy is via the marginal propensity to import. The 'structural approach' would argue that real expenditure decisions were responsive to wealth, monetary factors, expectations, etc., and that an essential part of the story of the balance of payments is to account for the variation of the private sector surplus which the neo-Cambridge theory assumes to be constant. A further, but clearly related, difference would be the neo-Cambridge preoccupation with Keynes's income-expenditure mechanism to the exclusion of Keynes's monetary theories which serve to constrain the income-expenditure mechanism and Keynes's theory of the capital account in the *Tract on Monetary Reform*, which in no way is overriden by his later work. In these respects, while claims to intellectual pedigree must inevitably be viewed with caution, the 'structural approach' owes a greater allegiance to the totality of Keynes's achievements in monetary and balance of payments theory in so far as it integrates his theories of forward market activity, income-expenditure in an open economy, and his monetary theory as later refined by the Yale School of financial theory, e.g. Hester and Tobin (eds) [1967], and its relationship to the macro-economy.

Finally, the 'structural approach', by explicitly recognising the market for money, generalises the arguments of the so-called Monetary Theory of the balance of payments. Interestingly enough, the conclusions of the neo-Cambridge Theory and the Monetary Theory in some respects are similar, although the intellectual routes along which these conclusions are reached are dissimilar in almost every respect. The essential tenet of the Monetary Theory, e.g. Johnson [1972], is that an excess supply of money in an open economy would be eliminated by a balance of payments deficit which would continue until the difference between the supply and the demand for money was eliminated.

The main conclusions of the Monetary Approach as developed more fully in Frenkel and Johnson [1976] are:

(*a*) When the exchange rate is fixed a balance of payments deficit for a small open economy is the process by which the economy adjusts to an excess supply of money. Since domestic interest rates are assumed to be determined by world interest rates and domestic prices by world prices, at the 'natural' rate of unemployment the only way in which an economy can adjust to an excess of liquidity is through the balance of payments.

(*b*) When the exchange rate is flexible, the domestic economy is insulated from overseas monetary developments. Under these circumstances the economy adjusts to an excess supply of money through an increase in the domestic price level and the exchange rate floats downwards to restore the original differential between the domestic and overseas price levels when expressed in the same currency.

Since the monetary authorities alone can create money, the 'monetarists' conclude that the authorities are responsible for balance of payments deficits when the exchange rate is fixed but the rate of inflation depends on overseas monetary developments. When the exchange rate is flexible, the authorities are responsible for domestic inflation. Therefore, what matters in the Monetary Approach is the way in which the public sector financial deficit is financed. If it is financed via credit creation the neo-Cambridge and 'monetarist' schools imply the same thing—a balance of payments deficit is generated. If it is financed by selling government debt to the private sector the Monetary Approach implies that there will be no balance of payments deficit, while the neo-Cambridge result will be unaltered.

In its most compact from, e.g. Johnson [1972], the Monetary Approach implicitly consolidates the markets for spot exchange and money by assuming that domestic and overseas output and financial assets are perfect substitutes. In this way domestic prices may never diverge from world prices and domestic interest rates may never diverge from world interest rates. Since these assumptions preclude the major adjustment processes to excess liquidity there is a danger of concluding that the Monetary Approach to the balance of payments is arrived at by default.

In this way, domestic interest rates cannot move out of line with world interest rates and the domestic price of traded goods cannot move out of line with world prices. Therefore in an open economy any change in the money supply could not raise the domestic price of traded goods by the assumption of perfect arbitrage in goods. Nor could it change domestic interest rates on the assumption that the demand for money was interest-elastic, since the arbitrageurs would always seek to equate domestic and world interest rates. When the exchange rate is fixed, only the balance of payments can equate the supply and demand for money. If the exchange rate is flexible, equilibrium is reached via a depreciation of the spot rate which enables domestic prices to rise and eliminate the excess supply of money while maintaining the equality of domestic and world prices in terms of the same currency.

Whether or not these extreme assumptions are justified is an essentially empirical issue upon which the 'structural approach' does not have a prior view. There is, however, an extensive body of evidence, e.g. Beenstock and Minford [1976], which confirms the approach developed by Armington [1969] that traded goods may be distinguished by their country of origin and that the elasticity of substitution between traded goods from different countries is less than infinite in both the short and long runs. The assumption of perfect arbitrage in traded goods therefore conflicts with this extensive body of evidence, at least over the observed range of relative price movements.

The assumption of perfect arbitrage in traded financial assets and liabilities is one of the key issues to which this study is directed. Here too the balance of the empirical evidence, as reported for example by Branson and Hill [1971] and Kouri and Porter [1974], is not sympathetic to the perfect arbitrage assumption. Argy and Hodjera [1973] in their study of international financial integration, conclude not surprisingly that while there is a substantial degree of international financial integration, it is less than perfect.

It will be argued that the assumptions of perfect substitution in internationally traded goods and financial assets are not central to the Monetary Approach and that when the exchange rate is fixed the domestic price level and interest rates are in the long run indirectly dependent on their overseas counterparts when both of these assumptions are relaxed. In other words the 'structural aproach' and the Monetary Approach are logically convergent. However, the relaxation of these assumptions will alter the dynamic structure of the long-term relationships postulated in the Monetary Approach. As it were, the long run becomes even longer the lower the elasticity of substitution between internationally traded goods and financial assets. This accords with intuition in the stock-flow framework of the 'structural approach', since the lower the elasticity of substitution the weaker are the linkages between the domestic and overseas economies.

Quite apart from the lags that are logically implied by the stock-flow mechanism in the 'structural approach', there will be additional lags in the behavioural relationships that make up the model. The more lags there are, the more time it will take for the long run to be reached. If the long run is in the remote future it may be argued by those that are prepared to accept the logic of the 'structural approach' and its 'monetarist'-like conclusions that they are irrelevant at the levels of policy making and applied economic forecasting. The policy implications of lags will be discussed at a later stage where it will be argued that the substantive issue for policy is not the length of the lags but the way in which macro-economic expectations about inflation, the exchange rate, interest rates, etc., are formed. There is a very real danger that policy makers will be tempted into playing a game that might be called 'beat the lags', where policy is designed to make the long run arrive sooner than it naturally would and destabilising in the economy in the process. If indeed the lags are long and expectations are formed rationally (in the sense of Muth [1961]) it will be maintained that the authorities will have to be extra-patient and that there is little at the macro-economic level than can be done. Instead a number of micro-economic issues are raised, since, if the efficiency of the individual markets that take up the macro-economy can be improved, lags may be reduced and the impact of macro-economic policy made more swift. For example, if capital and labour are made more mobile within the domestic economy, disequilibrium will be eliminated more quickly and the long run will be brought forward in time.

However, it is important to distinguish the lags in the real world from the very long and incredible lags that econometric models sometimes imply. In practice it is very difficult to estimate distributed lags using time series. In addition the modelling of expectations which are so crucial to the diagnostic structure of econometric models is at least equally hazardous. It frequently happens that simulations on large-scale econometric models indicate that when all the lag structures are convoluted, the long run is decades away—if not centuries—assuming that the model is stable in the first place. As will be emphasised later and as is implied by Muth [1961], even if the lag structures are long, provided knowledge about them is held with perfect certainty on the part of the market, the *ex-post* lag will be zero. If indeed it was thought that the effects of a policy would be to raise prices in a hundred years' time, and this belief was held with perfect certainty, prices would rise straight away. In other words, rational expectations have the effect of collapsing lag structures.

Policy Questions

In the foregoing discussion we have already touched upon a number of policy issues regarding the influence of the exchange rate and monetary policy on the balance of payments. We have also touched upon the influence of interest rates on the capital account. In this section we focus in somewhat greater detail on the range of policy issues discussed in the remainder of this book. Since we intend to deal with capital account matters and wider balance of payments issues somewhat separately, the policy issues are listed on the same basis.

(i) The Capital Account
Short-term Interest–Sensitivity.   The proposition that an increase in interest rates will generate inflows on the capital account of the balance of payments is familiar. Indeed most monetary authorities are very conscious of this, especially as a short-term balance of payments weapon. However, what the capital inflow is likely to be when domestic interest rates are raised by, say, one percentage point relative to overseas interest rates is a matter for considerable debate. Much of the empirical section of this volume is dedicated to trying to answer this question, based on a number of econometric studies of the capital accounts in the U.K., France and West Germany.

One school of thought argues that because a financial asset that is covered in the forward exchange market does not bear any exchange risk it should be a perfect substitute for an asset of comparable maturity that is denominated in some other currency. If this were the case, covered positions would be perfect substitutes for each other and, say, a one percentage point increase in the covered differential of a country would in principle call forth an enormous capital inflow on the balance of payments. We shall call this the perfect arbitrage school, since it implies that covered interest arbitrage would always eliminate any opening in the covered differential.

The reasons why in practice the covered differential may be non-zero have already been reviewed by Officer and Willet [1970]. One possibility is that covered assets are not a perfect substitute since (as the Herstatt failure of 1974 reminds us) default risk may still be present. The stance in the present study is to determine the responsiveness of the covered interest arbitrage schedule empirically. The main conclusion in these respects is that the responsiveness of covered arbitrage to changes in the covered differential in the light of the growing body of international evidence is surprisingly small.

The perfect arbitrage school which in its French idiom has been called 'Cambism' (see Spraos [1972]) does not, however, imply that the authorities may solve their balance of payments problems by altering domestic interest rates. An equally critical factor is the supply of forward cover which the covered interest arbitrageurs wish to buy. The forward exchange that is held by arbitrageurs has to be supplied by speculators in the forward exchange market or by the authorities who would be essentially speculating on behalf of the taxpayers. If the authorities agree to supply forward exchange on demand they could generate a larger inflow when they raise interest rates. In the absence of such a policy the speculative supply of forward exchange would constrain the arbitrage response on the capital account. Because forward exchange speculation is inherently risky the speculative supply of forward exchange may be inelastic. Subsequently, the responsiveness of short-term capital flows to changes in domestic interest rates (for given overseas interest rates) could be muted. An important aspect of the empirical work in this study is to measure this response. The basic conclusion is that it is small and that subsequently short-term capital flows are insensitive to changes in uncovered interest rate differentials. The empirical insensitivities of the arbitrage and speculation schedules combine to imply that the capital account is insensitive to changes in short-term interest rates. This insensitivity is explained in terms of an apparently high subjective evaluation of exchange risk and/or a high degree of risk aversion.

Long-term Interest–Sensitivity. The same issues apply at the long end of the capital account except that here there are usually no forward exchange markets. Subsequently, investors incur exchange risk directly and cannot contract it out to others. When the supply of exchange risk is taken into consideration there is no obvious reason why the sensitivity of the capital account to changes in long-term interest rate differentials should be much different from the short-term sensitivity. Indeed, some of the results reported support this proposition, although some of the econometric results raise more questions than they solve. Nevertheless, while it would seem that monetary authorities regard short-term interest rates as their main policy instrument regarding the capital account of the balance of payments, from the present study it would seem that the long-term end of the capital account is a neglected corner of monetary policy that might be as effective as short-term monetary policy.

The Effects of Forward Intervention. Various attempts are made empirically to measure the likely response of the capital account to official intervention in the forward exchange markets. Since one of the basic conclusions is that there is apparently a dearth of exchange risk-taking in the spot and forward exchange markets, official intervention, which is a form of supply of exchange risk-bearing on the part of the monetary authorities, may have significant effects on the capital account. Indeed, the results that are reported tend to confirm this picture, suggesting that official forward intervention will be largely reflected by arbitrage activity in the spot market. Therefore, forward intervention is a potentially powerful weapon at the disposal of the authorities provided it is used with care and wisdom, as discussed later.

It should be emphasised that the foregoing discussion is intended to be positive rather than normative. We merely summarise the effects of different policy measures on the capital account without necessarily suggesting that the various policies are desirable. To form a normative judgement involves wider considerations to which we turn next.

(ii) Wider Macro-economic Considerations
The Assignment of Policy. A theory of economic policy that was popular during the 1960s and which in certain circles is most probably still prevalent today was that independent policy instruments could be assigned to achieve different policy objectives. This approach, which stems from Tinbergen [1956], Mundell [1962], [1963] and others affords the authorities an impressive range of policies such as monetary and fiscal policies, the exchange rate, etc., which in principle at least enables the authorities to achieve many if not all of their major policy goals such as full employment, balance of payments equilibrium, price stability, etc., etc.

This activist approach to discretionary economic policies has more recently been reinforced by the optimal control approach to the formulation of macro-economic policy, e.g. Livesey [1971], Pindyck [1973], and Pitchford and Turnovsky (eds) [1977], which is essentially a dynamic version of the more familiar static approaches referred to in the previous paragraph. The control-theoretic approach to policy formulation takes into account the lagged effects that various discretionary policies might have on the economy.

These views on economic policy contrast starkly with a roughly contemporaneous development where it is argued that discretionary macro-economic policies are likely to be destabilising and counterproductive and that instead the authorities should in the main adhere to some form of policy rule. The most widely debated of these rules is one suggested by Friedman [1958] that the authorities should adhere to a prescribed growth in the money supply irrespective of macro-economic developments and that this is likely in the longer term to be the best guarantee of full employment and price stability.

In this context it would seem that there are two main issues to be unravelled. First, as will be argued in this book, it is most probably illusory to believe that in the long run independent policy weapons may successfully be assigned to achieve various policy objectives. Indeed it would seem that there is very little that the authorities may achieve with macro-economic policies other than to determine the general level of prices in the long run. Therefore, in a growing economy a monetary rule would have the desirable effect of generating price stability. Secondly, it may be argued that because of lags the long run may be remote, and that even if the authorities cannot influence much in the long run, through discretionary policies they might be able to speed up the rate at which the long run arrives. For example, they may be able to bring about the earlier arrival of full employment or equilibrium in the balance of payments. This is the game of 'beating the lags' to which reference has already been made. The issues in this context depend critically on the way in which macro-economic expectations are formulated as has been emphasised by Lucas [1972], [1976], Sargent and Wallace [1975] and others. It will be argued that if expectations are 'rational' there is no way in which 'beating the lags' can be productive, since the economy will already be on an optimal path. This study would suggest that there is little if any scope for discretionary policies to be applied successfully and that passive policy rules are desirable assuming the macro-economic structure that is postulated.

This debate raises a number of interesting questions in political economy, since the Keynesian Revolution has provided more than a generation of policy practitioners with the intellectual justification for an extensive degree of activism and political importance which they might be reluctant to give up. While the implementation of policy rules requires a considerable degree of administration, non-discretionary policies do not have the same political appeal to civil servants and politicians as do their discretionary counterparts. However, it is arguable that the U.S. authorities who were the first to embark on policies of Keynesian activism in the 1930s may also be the first to abandon them in favour of policy rules — as witnessed by the policies pursued by Arthur Burns since 1972 as Chairman of the Federal Reserve System.

Floating Exchange Rates. Especially since August 1971, when President Nixon broke the ties between gold and the U.S. dollar, the international financial community has experienced varying degrees of experimentation with floating exchange rates. While the instability feared by some of the anti-floaters has failed to materialise, the debate about floating is far from resolved. Many central banks have preferred managed to clean floating and there have been few if any cases of perfectly flexible exchange rates. In a real sense floating, like Christianity has never been tried.

It is argued in this book that the substantive issue in this debate is the way in which exchange rate expectations are determined. This becomes fairly apparent once it is realised that managed floating is essentially foreign exchange speculation on the part of the authorities; in which case

whether or not intervention in the foreign exchange markets is desirable
depends on whether or not the monetary authorities' views about the
appropriate exchange rate in the future are any better than those of the
market as a whole. If foreign exchange speculation is 'rational' the
exchange rate will be optimal in which case any intervention by the
monetary authorities would be unnecessary. Indeed, under these
circumstances managed floating would be inefficient.

Plan of Study

The remainder of this book is divided into two parts. Part A, 'Studies in
the Balance of Payments', concentrates on the wider, essentially
theoretical, issues regarding the balance of payments as a whole,
whereas Part B, 'Studies in International Financial Transactions'
discusses a number of empirical issues regarding the structure of
forward markets and the processes of international financial substitution. Chapter 2 sketches out what is meant by the 'structural
approach' to the balance of payments. The main intellectual building
blocks are introduced and discussed. Chapter 3 is essentially a
continuation of the previous chapter, where the various building blocks
are integrated and the subsequent analytical implications are explored.
In Chapter 4 a discussion about exchange rate expectations is presented.
This forms a dual purpose since as well as exploring a number of
normative issues that various models of exchange rate expectations
imply, the discussion suggests a specification for exchange rate expectations that may be developed in the econometric sections in Part B. In
Chapter 5 the policy issues of part A are summarised.

Part B begins with an empirical discussion in Chapter 6 of the
structure of forward exchange markets based on econometric studies for
the U.K., France, Germany and Canada. Chapter 7 discusses the
econometric modelling of short and long-term capital movements on the
basis of data for France, Germany and the U.K. The following chapter
explores what has hitherto been an almost completely neglected aspect
of the forward exchange market—the term structure of forward
exchange rates. A theoretical model is presented and explored and a
number of empirical estimates are discussed based on the £/$ term
structure of forward exchange rates. Chapter 9 explores some of the
international financial linkages between countries, based on a theoretical model of the euro-dollar market. It also presents some econometric
results regarding the determination of the euro-dollar deposit rate in the
context of a world system where the 'world' is defined as the U.S., U.K.,
France, West Germany and Canada. Chapter 10 summarises the policy
issues that arise out of Part B in their relationship with the first part of
the book.

PART A

STUDIES IN THE BALANCE OF PAYMENTS

2 A Macro-economic Frame-work for the Balance of Payments

In this chapter the various intellectual building blocks to be used in the discussion for the balance of payments in the next chapter are introduced. We begin by introducing a small set of real markets that would be relevant to the discussion. In particular the markets for exportables, import substitutes, imports and non-traded goods are cited. In addition the labour market is included in the analysis. In view of the discussions of the capital account in Part B of this book, the introduction of the markets for foreign exchange and especially the market for forward exchange and the determinants of capital account behaviour receive a more detailed treatment. Finally, the financial markets are introduced.

The concentration on the specification of markets is motivated by the belief that macro-economic behaviour is a complex of market interactions and that the maze of feedback effects may only be understood in terms of an appropriate set of market forces. However, non-neoclassical notions may be introduced into the market conception of the macro-economy without affecting the long-run logic implied by market forces, as will be discussed in the next chapter. Nevertheless, these notions will be relevant in the short run.

The theoretical developments that are suggested here extend the previous work of Argy and Porter [1972], Black [1973] and Basevi [1973] in several respects. The common feature of these studies is the integration of the domestic financial markets with the spot and forward markets, while explicitly recognising the current and capital account components of the balance of payments. Miller [1973] also integrates these markets in their relationship to the domestic U.K. monetary systems but concentrates his attention on the capital account alone. However, neither Black nor Basevi relates the current account to the spot rate, relative prices etc. Black [p. 9] effectively ignores the interaction of the current account with the general equilibrium system that he describes by assuming it to be predetermined. This assumption may be useful in a dynamic analysis, or to obtain recursiveness for econometric purposes. However, in a long-run static analysis the current account is unlikely to be invariant to the exchange rate.

Basevi [p. 112] does not describe how the current account is determined and how it interacts with the exchange rate in particular. Only Argy and Porter [p. 505] explicitly endogenise the current account alongside the capital account. However, their treatment of the forward market is deficient since they assume that the forward rate is determined exclusively by speculators and therefore that covered interest arbitrage may be ignored.

Hopefully, these shortcomings and omissions are rectified below. In addition the links between the markets for traded goods, non-traded goods and money that have been discussed by Dornbusch [1973] are included in the analysis. However, we drop the extreme assumption of a perfect elasticity of substitution between traded output from different countries on the grounds that the alternative approach suggested by Armington [1969] in both the short and long run enjoys a greater degree of empirical support.

Having specified the structure of the macro-economy of which the balance of payments is an integral part, we are in a position to analyse how through this structure the balance of payments, *inter alia*, will be determined. This is the essence of the 'structural approach.'

The Real Markets

We begin with the balance of payments identity which, as pointed out in the previous chapter, may be considered as the excess demand for spot exchange. The change in the reserves will equal exports minus imports plus long and short-term capital flows:

$$\Delta RES \equiv X \cdot P_x - M \cdot \frac{P_x}{S} + STC + LTC \qquad (2.1)$$

where ΔRES = reserve change
X = volume of exports
P_x = price of exports in domestic currency
M = volume of imports
P_m = price of imports in foreign currency
S = spot rate (units of foreign currency per unit of domestic currency)
STC = short-term capital flows
LTC = long-term capital flows

Having established this identity we proceed by demonstrating how each of the variables on the right-hand side of equation 2.1 is determined in the context of a general equilibrium model of the macro-economy. The real domestic economy is assumed to produce exportables, import substitutes and non-traded goods. Each of these markets will include supply and demand components with relative prices and interest rates as the key explanatory variables.

We may begin by considering the market for exportables. The supply of exportables (XS) in the long run will depend on productive potential (Q) and the profitability on the production of exportables relative to the production of import substitutes and non-traded output. Thus:

$$XS = XS(\overset{+}{Q}, \overset{+}{P}_x, \bar{P}_{ms}, \bar{P}_n) \qquad (2.2)$$

where P_{ms} and P_n are the prices of import substitutes and non-traded goods respectively. The signs of the partial derivatives are shown above the variables to which they refer. An increase in aggregate output will, *ceteris paribus*, add to the supply of exportables and an increase in P_x on the same basis would raise profitability on the production of exportables and resources would be transferred into the production of exportables. The opposite would be true if competing prices rose, *ceteris paribus*.

The demand for exportables would have a foreign and domestic component. The foreign demand would depend positively on the volume of world trade (WT), and negatively on competitiveness. Hence:

$$X = X(\overset{+}{W}T, \bar{P}_x, \bar{S}, \overset{+}{P}_{xw}) \qquad (2.3)$$

where P_{xw} is the price of exportables overseas. The assumption that the derivatives of X with respect to the components of competitiveness, i.e. P_x, S, and P_{xw} are less than infinite, is based on the approach of Armington [1969].

The approach to the allocation of domestic demand recognises that first a choice must be made between the accumulation of real rather than financial assets which in this presentation includes money (L) and bonds, both short (BS) and long-term (BL). This decision is assumed to depend on real interest rates. Secondly, given the decision to spend rather than to accumulate financial assets, a decision must be made on the allocation of this real expenditure across the three domestic outputs and imports. This decision is assumed to depend on relative prices in the long run. Therefore, the demand by residents for exportable output may be hypothesised as:

$$XD = XD(\overset{+}{Y}, \bar{r}_s, \bar{r}_L, \overset{+}{x}, \overset{+}{P}_{ms}, \bar{P}_x, \overset{+}{P}_m, \bar{S}, \overset{+}{P}_n) + E_x \qquad (2.4)$$

where x is the anticipated rate of inflation and Y is real (disposable) income and is defined as actual rather than potential output.

$$Y = XS + N + MS \qquad (2.5)$$

where N and MS denote actual outputs of non-traded goods and import substitutes respectively. E_x denotes government expenditure on exportables. In the longer run Y should equal Q, but in the shorter run they could differ. More appropriately equation 2.4 should specify permanent income as a proxy for the discounted value on human capital, in which case it would have been meaningful to specify Q rather than Y, but this distinction is unimportant in the present context.

We close the market for exportables by writing

$$XS = X + XD \tag{2.6}$$

as the market clearing condition and this will determine P_x and X in equation 2.1. Equation 2.6 is of course a long-run condition. Protracted adjustment processes and the gradual elimination of excess demand may of course be more realistic at the empirical level. A discussion of these and related issues may be found in Hutton and Minford [1975]. This caveat indeed may be extended to all the arguments that follow which are expressed in long-run equilibrium format.

We may now write the conditions for equilibrium in the markets for import substitutes and non-traded goods as:

$$MS(\overset{+}{Q}, \overset{+}{P}_{ms}, \bar{P}_n, \bar{P}_x) = MSD(\overset{+}{Y}, \bar{r}_s, \bar{r}_L, \overset{+}{x}, \overset{+}{P}_n, \bar{P}_{ms}, \overset{+}{P}_x, \overset{+}{P}_m, \bar{S}) + E_{ms} \tag{2.7}$$

$$N(\overset{+}{Q}, \bar{P}_{ms}, \overset{+}{P}_n, \bar{P}_x) = ND(\overset{+}{Y}, \bar{r}_s, \bar{r}_L, \overset{+}{x}, \bar{P}_{ms}, \overset{+}{P}_x, \bar{P}_m, \bar{P}_n, \bar{S}) + E_x \tag{2.8}$$

where MSD and ND are the two demand components. A condition on the partial derivatives would be that the elasticity of substitution (in demand) between import substitutes and imports would be greater than the elasticities of substitution between these products and the other products. Similarly, it would be reasonable to assume that higher elasticities of substitution existed between traded goods than between traded and non-traded goods. E_{ms} denotes government expenditure on import substitutes and E_n on non-traded output.

The current account is completed by determining the demand for imports, which may be written as

$$M = M(\overset{+}{Y}, \bar{r}_s, \bar{r}_L, \overset{+}{x}; \bar{P}_m, \overset{+}{S}, \overset{+}{P}_{ms}, \overset{+}{P}_n, \overset{+}{P}_x) \tag{2.9}$$

i.e. the marginal propensity to import operates alongside neo-classical notions of price sensitivity. The monetary variables have yet to be determined, but S, P_{ms}, P_n and P_x have all been determined in the model that has been described so far. The price of imports is assumed to be exogenous.

For simplicity it has been assumed that costs are homogeneous across all activities – hence relative profitability depended on relative prices alone. Aggregate costs will be reflected in aggregate output. If costs rise, then for given prices Q is likely to fall. If, on the other hand, real aggregate profits are unchanged then Q is likely to be unchanged. In the present model three varieties of costs may be identified – unit labour costs (W), unit import costs and capital costs, i.e. real borrowing costs. Thus:

$$Q = Q(\overset{+}{P}_n, \overset{+}{P}_{ms}, \overset{+}{P}_x; \bar{W}; \bar{P}_m, \overset{+}{S}; \bar{r}_s, \bar{r}_L, \bar{x}) \qquad (2.10)$$

may be considered as the aggregate supply curve of productive potential. If this supply curve shifts to the left on account of an increase in unit costs, e.g. wage costs, then for given demand, i.e. if monetary policy is perfectly accommodating, prices will rise in similar proportions. If monetary policy is not assumed to be accommodating with respect to the increase in costs and aggregate demand is price-elastic, e.g. via the real balance effect, domestic prices will rise proportionately less than the increase in costs and real output will fall.

To close this part of the 'structural approach' we specify a real or augmented Phillips Curve where excess demand in the labour market is taken to depend on the difference between demand and aggregate supply. With the exception of this modification we may therefore determine wage costs along familiar lines, where cost inflation depends on the pressure of demand and the expected rate of inflation:

$$\frac{\Delta W}{W} = \overset{+}{W}(\bar{Q}; \overset{+}{Y}, \overset{+}{x}) \qquad (2.11)$$

Our purpose here is not to provide a detailed treatment of factor demand theory and the Phillips hypothesis. Our intention is rather to close the system, having completed a detailed outline of the interaction between the markets for non-traded goods and traded output in their relationship with the current account of the balance of payments. A detailed discussion of the issues here may be found in Phelps (ed.) [1971].

We now describe a conceptual experiment where the spot rate has depreciated in order to illustrate the mechanics of the framework that has been so far described. Inevitably, what we have to say at this stage will be of a partial equilibrium nature since we have to specify the financial and forward markets. However, in the next chapter we shall repeat the same conceptual experiment in a full general equilibrium manner.

A fall in the spot rate will in the first instance cause the balance of payments to deteriorate since via equation 2.1 import prices in domestic currency will rise proportionately. The fall in the spot rate would also generate additional export demand via equation 2.3 and reduce import demand via equation 2.9. Even if the Marshall-Lerner conditions are eventually fulfilled, protracted adjustment processes would suggest a J-shaped response of the current account to the exchange rate depreciation, i.e. initially because of higher import prices the current account measured in domestic currency units deteriorates. Eventually, however, this deterioration is more than offset by the import and export elasticities. In what follows, however, we concern ourselves with long-run equilibria only, in which case the J-curve may be ignored.

The increase in export demand from overseas will raise the price of exportables. Similarly, the reduction in the demand for imports will be accompanied by an increase in the demand for import substitutes in particular. Resources will therefore be transferred out of the non-traded goods sector into import substitutes and exportables. The increase in the domestic price of exportables would be proportionately lower than the rate of depreciation, in which case both the physical quantity of exports (X) and their price will have increased and the balance of payments improved.

The depreciation will also raise domestic costs both directly and indirectly. The direct effect is higher import costs which *ceteris paribus* would be reflected in higher prices, the precise degree depending on the 'coerciveness' of monetary policy. However, because the value added of imports is a fraction of the total value added, the inflationary consequences of the depreciation cannot be self-defeating. More important are the indirect effects via higher unit labour costs since labour will tend to account for the vast majority of value added. To the extent that higher prices will be reflected by higher wages through equation 2.11 which in turn via equation 2.10 would add to cost inflation, a depreciation could be self-defeating if (a) the proportional value added of imports and labour in GDP were unity; and, perhaps more importantly, (b) if the authorities permitted through an accommodating monetary policy the increase in unit import costs to be reflected in the higher prices which ignite the countervailing wage-price spiral that has just been described. Thus a condition for self-defeat is that a 1 per cent increase in prices is eventually compensated by a 1 per cent increase in wages. These issues are further discussed in the ensuing chapters.

The cost syndrome and the resource and demand reallocation syndromes that are ignited by the change in the exchange rate take place simultaneously. The generalised partial equilibrium Marshall-Lerner conditions for an improvement of the current account are exceedingly complicated. A further complication is that if monetary policy is not accommodating domestic demand will fall. Where it falls and by how much is essentially an empirical issue. Yet it is empirical questions of this nature which are likely to have a significant bearing on the final answer. Although the multiplicity of interactions creates the impression that the progress of the macro-economy would be difficult to foresee, in the next chapter we show that in the long run the situation is considerably more simple. In the short run, however, the complexity is real enough and it may be the case that for a while at least the economy may react perversely to policy stimuli.

Foreign Exchange Markets

While in any general equilibrium analysis the separation of different markets must inevitably be to some degree arbitrary, as an exegetical procedure it seems reasonable to discuss the foreign exchange markets, spot and forward under a separate heading. Likewise it seemed reasonable to discuss the real markets under a separate heading, and in the next section the interactions with the domestic financial markets are discussed. In what follows, we discuss the interactions of the spot and forward markets in so far as they are related through the capital account. That is to say, for the moment, we abstract from the current account and its influence on the foreign exchange markets. These and other interactions will be brought together in the next chapter. A further crucial interaction will be the role of speculation and expectations about the exchange rate, which must be regarded as an integral component of the 'structural approach' and which is closely related to the overall model that has been described. These issues are, however, deferred to Chapter 4, since they warrant a treatment of their own. For expositional purposes, we consider only one forward market. (The micro- and macro-economic theory of multiple forward markets is developed in Chapter 8.) The analysis is presented in linear format since one of our objectives is to derive estimable equations for Part B.

Forward and spot market transactions are inextricably interwoven through the existence of covered interest arbitrage. In what follows, we outline the theoretical links between the spot and forward markets, identify the role of speculative activity both spot and forward, and demonstrate the role of official forward intervention in the foreign exchange markets.

We begin by recalling some of the key theoretical properties of the Tobin-Markowitz portfolio selection model which forms the ideological basis for most of what follows. Most important of these is the conclusion that elasticities are a function of the expected variance-covariance structure of the set of expected yields. If future outcomes were expected with absolute certainty, elasticities would be infinite at positive rates of return for there would be no risk attached to investment. It is the presence of risk and the aversion to risk that bounds the scale of investment decisions in generating finite elasticities. This forms the basis for a world where yields may actually differ, which of course would conflict with the infinite elasticity assumption. Therefore the elasticity of speculation would tend to be finite. More troublesome is the elasticity of the covered interest arbitrage schedule where exchange risks are zero. If indeed there were no other risks, one would expect an infinitely elastic arbitrage schedule. However, default risks would remain (e.g. Herstatt) and one would therefore expect a high but not necessarily infinitely elastic arbitrage schedule.

The position assumed in the present study is that the elasticity of the arbitrage and speculation schedules is essentially an empirical issue. Whereas in the theory of demand for goods one is essentially concerned with estimating the elasticities of substitution between goods, in financial theory one is essentially concerned with the estimation of the variance-covariance matrix of returns on different risky assets since portfolio theory suggests that it is upon such factors, as well as the extent of risk aversion, that the actual *ex post* substitution of alternative financial assets depends. Both these factors are empirical phenomena about which we might have *a priori* expectations, but the proof of the pudding is in the eating.

A popular school of thought primarily associated with the Cambists (see p. 18) is that the covered arbitrage schedule is infinitely elastic, in which case the covered differential should tend to zero. The Cambists would insist that speculative activity in the forward market or for that matter official forward intervention, could not affect the forward rate since it is dominated by covered interest arbitrage. Any forward rate that did not set the covered differential to zero would instantaneously invite an infinite degree of inward or outward arbitrage switching in the forward market. The basis for this argument would be that a covered position in currency A is a perfect substitute for a covered position in any other currency because all exchange risk is avoided. Since the short-term assets and liabilities that are involved, e.g. three-month bank deposits, Treasury Bills, etc., are capital-certain, all risks are absent or removed; in which case, the argument goes, the covered interest arbitrage schedule should be infinitely elastic at the forward rate which sets the covered differential to zero.

A modification of this view, e.g. Frenkel and Levitch [1975], is that because of brokerage and other transactions costs there may be a zone of indeterminacy in between which the forward rate may move without attracting large-scale (if any) orders for forward exchange from covered-interest arbitrageurs. This argument is analogous to the gold points of the classical theory of the gold standard. However, beyond this zone the arbitrage schedule is infinitely elastic once more.

A more hybrid approach, e.g. Spraos [1972], is that Cambism may on the whole be realistic when speculation is not rife. However, during speculative crises, speculators may be able to exert considerable pressure on the forward rate. The difficulty with this argument, even in the context of its own terms of reference, is that if it is the risklessness of covered interest arbitrage that causes the forward rate to be determined on an outright basis by covered interest arbitrage the same should be true during periods of speculation. Large-scale speculative forward sales should be immediately taken up by arbitrageurs and therefore reflected in the spot market. There is no obvious reason why covered interest arbitrage should be any riskier during a speculative crisis than at any other time.

The Modern Theory of forward exchange as articulated by Jasay [1958] and Tsiang [1959] suggests that in general neither the speculation schedule nor the arbitrage schedule need be infinitely elastic. (Indeed, if they are both infinitely elastic the forward rate would be indeterminate.) Officer and Willett [1970] have already reviewed the diverse reasons why the arbitrage schedule may be less than perfectly elastic. It is merely added here that as long as some risk exists (and the Herstatt failure of 1974 indicates that default risks cannot be ruled out) the degree of inelasticity of the arbitrage schedule would depend on risk-aversion. A small element of risk with a high element of risk-aversion could imply a fairly low covered-interest arbitrage elasticity.

To repeat, the standpoint of the present study is essentially that of the Modern Theory and how elastic or inelastic the various schedules may be is to be determined, in so far as this is possible, on an empirical basis.

In the long and sometimes heated debate over whether the covered-interest arbitrage schedule is infinitely elastic or not, it would appear that perhaps the main issue has got lost. What is important to the balance of payments and policy is not so much whether the arbitrage schedule is infinitely elastic or not, but rather, whatever its elasticity may be, how much forward cover will be available to covered-interest arbitrage when for example domestic interest rates change. In other words, it is the absolute elasticity of the speculation schedule which is important, the relative weights of arbitrage to speculation, the subject of the studies by Stoll [1968], Kesselman [1971] and Spraos [1972] being of less practical concern. If, for example, the covered-interest arbitrage schedule were infinitely elastic at the forward rate which sets the covered differential to zero and the authorities raised domestic interest rates, spot transactions (assuming the spot rate to be fixed) would depend on the speculative supply of forward exchange at the new forward rate. If the speculative schedule were infinitely inelastic there could be no spot transactions. On the other hand, if the speculation schedule were infinitely elastic there would be an infinite spot inflow. The policy maker is therefore concerned in ascertaining the elasticities of both schedules. As we shall see, this information will provide him with guidance on the effects of official forward operations on the spot market.

In what follows, we operate with respect to a single domestic interest rate (r_d) which typically is represented by a short-term interest rate (r_s) and an overseas interest rate (r_w) of comparable maturity, etc. The forward rate (F) is of the same maturity as the interest rate to which it refers. The arbitrage demand for forward domestic currency is:

$$A_F = \alpha(r_w - r_d + S - F) \tag{2.12}$$

where the spot and forward rates have been normalised with respect to the interest rates (see p. 83).

S − F is the cost of forward cover and the expression in brackets is the covered differential expressed in favour of the home country. The speculative demand is assumed to respond to the difference between the expected spot rate (S^e) and the forward rate, i.e. the return on forward speculation:

$$Z_F = \beta(S^e - F) \tag{2.13}$$

In equilibrium the excess demand for forward exchange must sum to zero including the official forward position (G).

$$A_F + Z_F + G = 0 \tag{2.14}$$

in which case the equilibrium forward rate may be written as:

$$F = \frac{\alpha}{\alpha + \beta}(r_w - r_d + S) + \frac{\beta}{\alpha + \beta}S^e + \frac{1}{\alpha + \beta}G \tag{2.15}$$

Notice that the official forward position identifies the parameters α and β, the slopes of the arbitrage and speculation schedules respectively.

Short-term capital flows (STC) will be the sum of covered and uncovered (AU) interest arbitrage.

$$STC = -\Delta A_F + \Delta AU \tag{2.16}$$

where uncovered arbitrage (AU) responds to the expected interest rate differential:

$$AU = \gamma(r_d - r_w - S + S^e) \tag{2.17}$$

Since portfolio responses are likely to vary inversely with risk and since covered arbitrage does not involve any exchange risk, γ is likely to be smaller than α. Substituting equation 2.17 and 2.12 into equation 2.16 implies the following equation for short-term capital flows:

$$STC = -\alpha\Delta CFC + (\alpha + \gamma)\Delta UD + \gamma\Delta S^e - \gamma\Delta S \tag{2.18}$$

where UD and CFC are the uncovered differential and the cost of forward cover respectively, i.e.:

$$\left.\begin{array}{l} CFC = S - F \\ UD = r_d - r_w \end{array}\right\} \tag{2.19}$$

Substituting further from equation 2.15 into equation 2.18 implies the following reduced-form expression for short-term capital flows:

$$STC = \left(\frac{\alpha\beta}{\alpha + \beta} + \gamma\right)(\Delta UD - \Delta S + \Delta S^e)$$

$$+ \frac{\alpha}{\alpha + \beta}\Delta G \tag{2.20}$$

An increase in domestic interest rates raises the demand for domestic currency spot and lowers the demand for domestic currency forward. If the spot rate is fixed and the authorities do not intervene forward, covered spot transactions will take place only to the extent that speculators are prepared to sell foreign currency forward. If the speculation schedule is inelastic the spot flows will be reduced. This argument would not affect uncovered transactions. If the spot rate is flexible and the supply of spot exchange is inelastic, the effect would be to bid up the spot rate and the forward rate would not be affected. Indeed under these circumstances the forward rate would entirely reflect the speculative demand for forward exchange. Equal and opposite arguments would apply in the case of a rise in world interest rates. If the arbitrage schedule is infinitely elastic the covered differential would always be zero in equilibrium. Nevertheless, spot transactions would take place since the lower forward rate implies that speculators are selling forward exchange to arbitrageurs under the assumption that the expected spot rate is unaltered.

If the forward rate is dominated by arbitrageurs i.e. if $\alpha/(\alpha + \beta)$ equals unity it is clear that official sales of foreign currency forward will be bought by arbitrageurs in which case these sales will be reflected in reserve increases. Therefore the higher the elasticity of the arbitrage schedule relative to that of the speculation schedule, the greater the response of the reserves to official forward intervention; capital flows may be influenced in a way that does not involve domestic monetary policy.

Spot speculation or uncovered arbitrage is largely an irrational phenomenon and has been included in this presentation for the sake of completeness. If a speculator wishes to take a position against a currency he may do so by selling the currency forward in the hope of buying it back spot more cheaply without committing any actual spot funds and forgoing interest as would be the case with spot speculation. If, however, the forward rate has been driven down in line with speculative expectations but the spot rate, because of official operations, has not adjusted to these forward sales, speculators would stand to benefit (in expected value terms) by speculating spot too. Alternatively, exchange controls may prevent full access to forward markets in which case speculative activity may be deflected to the spot market from the forward market where it would otherwise have taken place. Some components of 'leads and lags' may be attributable to such factors. However, if a unit of domestic currency is sold forward rather than spot, it will be purchased by an arbitrageur who in any case would have sold spot in order to complete the implied covered transaction.

There may have been some confusion in the literature concerning the insulation of the domestic monetary system from the balance of payments and capital markets, in particular if the spot rate is flexible.

The standard argument runs that if domestic interest rates rise and the exchange rate is floating only the ownership of existing domestic currency positions net will alter. The increase in the overseas demand for domestic currency positions will bid up the exchange rate. This would coax residents, e.g. traders, to supply domestic currency to overseas investors, leaving the total stock of domestic currency positions unaltered. In contrast, if the exchange rates were fixed, the increase in domestic interest rates would add to the stock of high-powered money and increase the supply of money. Regardless of the elasticity of substitution between internationally traded financial assets and liabilities, the argument concludes that a floating spot rate insulates domestic monetary policy from world monetary forces.

While in itself this argument cannot be faulted it may be the case that even when the spot rate is pegged the domestic economy will be insulated from at least some overseas monetary influences. If international capital movements take place on a covered basis and the spot rate is fixed, the flexibility of the forward rate would tend to choke off short-term capital inflows if the authorities were to raise domestic interest or if world interest rates were to alter. In the limit, if the elasticity of supply of speculative forward cover were zero, i.e. if $\beta = 0$ the forward rate would tend to insulate domestic monetary policy from world monetary forces very much in the same way as the spot rate would according to the arguments of the previous paragraph. This degree of insulation varies inversely with both α and β. However, the forward rate cannot insulate the domestic economy from speculative, current account or long-term capital transactions.

However, it would be misleading to imply that it is the existence of the forward market that generates a degree of insulation that would otherwise be absent. The existence of the forward market creates a facility for the international investor and thereby increases the options that face him. It is necessary to take account of the exchange risks which in the absence of the forward market would tend to make internationally traded assets poor substitutes for each other. Therefore, if domestic interest rates were to rise relative to world rates, it would be unlikely that the domestic financial market would become flooded on account of short-term capital movements. There would of course tend to be some response but not enough effectively to integrate the domestic with the world capital market. If β were very large, i.e. if the speculative elasticity of supply of forward exchange were high, capital markets would tend to be more highly integrated. A highly elastic covered-interest arbitrage schedule is therefore only a necessary but not a sufficient condition for a high degree of capital market integration. An additional condition is a relatively elastic speculation schedule.

Forward exchange markets tend to be associated with fairly short-term maturities. The three-month maturity tends to be the most highly quoted, but the *Financial Times* quotes up to the twelve-month maturity on a daily basis. Long-term capital transactions must therefore be carried out without the facility of forward cover. Consequently, long-term capital flows would tend to be determined by the change in the subjective long-term covered differential, i.e. where long-term investors have, as it were, to supply their own cover in terms of the expected change in the exchange rate over the holding period:

$$LTC = \delta\Delta(r_{Ld} - r_{Lw} - S + S_L^e) \tag{2.21}$$

Notice that S^e in equation 2.17, for example, refers to a shorter forecasting horizon than S^e_L in equation 2.21 on account of the different holding periods.

Domestic Financial Markets

In what follows, three financial markets are considered: bonds, bills and money. Their role in the 'structural approach' is essentially to link the capital account with the real markets and hence the current account. A further vital role is the nexus between domestic monetary and fiscal policy and the balance of payments.

The change in the domestic money supply (ΔL) has two primary origins in terms of high-powered money. First the authorities may finance their borrowing requirement or budget deficit (BR) by selling short-term securities (GS), i.e. bills, or long-term securities (GL), i.e. bonds. Finally they may opt to print money (ΔL). We therefore have an identity of the form:

$$BR \equiv \Delta(GS + GL + L) \tag{2.22}$$

In this presentation we consolidate the banking sector with the domestic sector as a whole for the sake of simplicity and without losing any generality. However, Miller [1973] and Brunner [1973] develop much more detailed analyses of the interactions between the balance of payments and the domestic financial system. Therefore, in this presentation domestic credit expansion takes place through the unsophisticated process of the printing press. More usually, the authorities sell bonds to the banks which are financed through the creation of reserve assets. In equilibrium the expansion of bank assets must be matched by an expansion of bank liabilities, i.e. bank deposits which add to the money supply. The borrowing requirement is the difference between the revenue the exchequer obtains through taxation, duties, etc. (REV) and its expenditures both above and below the lines. In our highly simplified presentation these are the value of public expenditure and the purchases of foreign currency:

$$BR \equiv E.P + \Delta RES - REV \qquad (2.23)$$

While this is obviously not the place for a discussion of the very complicated relationship which in practice exists between the borrowing requirement and various macro-economic aggregates, a number of issues may be borne in mind. First, when public expenditure is fixed in real terms (i.e. E is fixed) inflation will tend to increase the borrowing requirement since the monetary value of public expenditure will be increased. On the other hand, revenue may increase too in the absence of indexation through progressive income tax structures as inflation sucks people into higher tax brackets. Subsequently, the effects of inflation on the borrowing requirement are indeterminate. Secondly, it is sometimes argued that an expansion of public expenditure will not increase the borrowing requirement since it will generate a higher tax take if economic activity is stimulated. However, it should also be recalled that any such expansionary efforts would tend to weaken the balance of payments and by running down the reserves the authorities would need to borrow less.

Official borrowing from overseas in foreign currency cannot reduce the overall borrowing requirement since this foreign currency must be converted into domestic currency. Alternatively a resident who receives foreign exchange which he converts into domestic currency at a fixed exchange rate will involve the authorities in official purchases of this foreign exchange. However, the authorities will have to borrow domestic currency to buy this foreign exchange. Hence the inclusion of the change in the reserves in equation 2.23. Once again the authorities will have to choose how to finance the purchase of the foreign exchange from residents. If they borrow they would effectively be borrowing the domestic currency proceeds of the foreign exchange from residents. However, residents would presumably only agree to this at a higher rate of interest. At the other extreme, the authorities may finance the purchase of foreign exchange by printing money. The authorities are therefore in a position to neutralise or sterilise inflows and outflows on the balance of payments. This may involve higher interest rates which would attract capital inflows and hence a further increase in the borrowing requirement. But as long as the speculative supply of forward exchange is inelastic a bounded sterilisation policy would tend to exist.

The previous discussion draws attention to the point that the principal policy consideration is the financing of the borrowing requirement rather than the borrowing requirement *per se*. If public expenditure increases, then as long as it is financed in an orthodox fashion through taxation or sales of debt to the private sector the monetary effects should be neutralised. Similarly, a strengthening of the balance of payments will only increase the domestic money supply if the authorities allow this to happen. If the authorities borrow from the private sector to buy the foreign exchange there will be no monetary effects and the reserve increase will have been sterilised. In practice, as we shall see, there may be limits to the authorities' sterilisation capacities. The more substantive long-term issues arising out of public expenditure are the effects on economic growth of a large participation of the public sector the economy. However, these issues are not discussed here.

So much for the supply of money. The demand for money (LD) will depend on prices, real incomes and interest rates:

$$LD = LD(\overset{+}{P}_x, \overset{+}{P}_{ms}, \overset{+}{P}_m, \overset{+}{P}_n, \bar{S}, \bar{r}_s, \bar{r}_L, \overset{+}{Y}) \tag{2.24}$$

The spot rate has a negative sign because an appreciation reduces import prices and therefore the demand for nominal balances. The market for money will be in equilibrium when

$$LD = L \tag{2.25}$$

For further discussion see Laidler [1969].

The demand functions for bills and bonds will depend on overseas and domestic factors. If for example there is a short term capital inflow net there will be a build-up of domestic bill holdings. Apart from this the demand for bills will depend on the relative rate of interest between bills and bonds. Writing the demand for bills in first difference we have:

$$\Delta GSD = GSD(\Delta \dot{r}_s, \Delta \bar{r}_L, \Delta \bar{P}) + STC \tag{2.26}$$

In equilibrium the change in the supply of bills must equal the change demand:

$$\Delta GS = \Delta GSD \tag{2.27}$$

Similarly, the bond market may be considered to be made up of domestic and overseas demand components where the latter is given by long-term capital flows. Analogous to equations 2.26 and 2.27 we therefore have:

$$\Delta GLD = GLD(\Delta \dot{r}_S, \Delta \bar{r}_L, \Delta \bar{P}) + LTC \tag{2.28}$$

$$\Delta GL = \Delta GLD \tag{2.29}$$

Notice that the demand for bills and bonds varies inversely with the vector of prices P. An increase in P, *ceteris paribus*, would reduce real balances and at the margin individuals would tend to run down their holdings of bills and bonds in order to add to their nominal money balances. Of course, by Walras' Law one market will be redundant. In the next chapter, we in fact 'eliminate' the market for bills.

No attempt is made here to discuss the term structure issues that are relevant to the interactions between the bill and bond markets. Our purpose here is simply to describe the main linkages in the 'structural approach' – the essential channels through which the markets for spot exchange, forward exchange, bills, bonds and real goods are likely to relate to one another.

The financial markets act as the bridge between the balance of payments and the real markets and vice versa. Consider for example the chain of reactions that is triggered off by a fall in world interest rates at the short end. In what follows we consider the situation as the logical stages unfold:

(a) the fall in r_w via equation 2.12 raises the covered arbitrage demand for bills. The amount of bills that are purchased will depend in the first instance on the supply of forward cover that is implied by equation 2.13. However the forward rate will fall via equation 2.15.
(b) Uncovered arbitrage will be induced via equation 2.17 and through equation 2.16 there will be a short-term capital inflow.
(c) If the spot rate is fixed the reserves will increase via equation 2.1. If the spot rate is flexible, any improvement on the capital account will be matched by an equal and opposite deterioration in the current account — i.e. the spot rate will be bid upwards. We first take up the story for when the spot rate is fixed.
(d) The increase in the reserves raises the borrowing requirement via equation 2.23 which if financed by an expansion of the money supply would tend to lower interest rates which in turn via equations 2.4, 2.7, 2.8 and 2.10 would raise prices through the process of excess demand creation. Alternatively the real balance effect may operate directly on prices. This in itself would tend to raise the demand for money in the direction of the increased supply. Also the lower domestic interest rates would generate some degree of equilibrating short and long-term capital outflow.
(e) The increase in domestic prices in general (ignoring any possible distributional effects on supply and demand) would increase the price of exports which through equation 2.3 would reduce the overseas demand for exports. Also import demand would rise via equation 2.9 and the current account would tend to deteriorate as a result, and the reserves would tend to fall.
(f) If the authorities financed additional borrowing requirement by selling bills to equal the increase in the reserves, the domestic economy, both money and subsequently real, would remain insulated. The money supply remains unchanged, therefore so do interest rates, prices, etc. Alternatively the same argument may be considered in terms of the bill market rather than the market for money. An increase in the demand for bills has been matched by an increase in the supply, so that the rate of interest on bills is unchanged. However, bills being an asset of domestic currency denomination, the reserves increase without affecting the money supply.
(g) Assuming that the authorities do not peg the exchange rate, a fall

in the world interest rate would raise the demand for domestic currency according to stages (*a*) and (*b*) and the spot rate will be bid up as in stage (*c*). The current account will have deteriorated and the capital account improved.

(*h*) Assuming that the supply of foreign exchange from the current account is not infinitely inelastic the total demand for bills will have risen in the first instance and this in principle will tend to have a depressing effect on the bill rate. However, the supply of money being unchanged, interest rates will be unchanged. The higher spot rate will reduce import costs and consequently domestic prices through equation 2.10, which would tend to reduce the demand for money, thereby lowering domestic interest rates in an equilibrating fashion. At the end of the day, the spot rate is bid up, the forward rate is bid down and domestic interest rates bid down to restore the covered differential to its equilibrium level.

These conceptual experiments hopefully foster a familiarity with the linkages between the intellectual building blocks that have been proposed. Having specified all the markets and identities, the world is logically complete in the sense that we now have a general equilibrium system in which all the basic economic aggregates that have been discussed may be logically determined. In the next chapter, the logic of this model is explored with particular emphasis on its long-term characteristics.

3 The Balance of Payments in the Long Run

The model that has been proposed in the previous chapter is intended to be generic of what might be called the mainstream of large-scale econometric models of open economies. Most probably a considerable proportion of model builders would regard the various building blocks as being desirable components in terms of model design, but in practice estimation difficulties, may prevent these sectors from being satisfactorily completed. For example, relatively few models incorporate capital account sectors, and even though a growing number of models are incorporating monetary sectors it is often the case that the financial structure of econometric models is more primitive than the income-expenditure structure.

No attempt has been made at discussing the details of these intellectual building blocks, which have largely been based on previous theoretical developments. The purpose of the present chapter is to integrate them and to investigate the logical long-run consequences as far as the balance of payments in particular is concerned. This is the essence of the 'structural approach'. However, at a small additional cost, a number of the important macro-economic aggregates are discussed; especially employment, interest rates and the general level of prices.

If the model that has been proposed is not controversial, as is intended to be the case, its logical consequences should not be controversial either. However, many of these consequences bear a close affinity with a number of 'monetarist' propensities, and there are many who would regard these as controversial enough. Hopefully, therefore, a contribution of the following discussion will be a narrowing of the divergence of some opinions in this area. At least an intellectual framework will have been formulated to work out the logical basis for these divergences of opinion.

To these and related ends the model discussed in the previous chapter is simplified slightly and linearised for expositional purposes. For example, the markets for non-traded output and import substitutes are consolidated into domestic output and we assume a single bond market instead of independent markets for bills and bonds. However, these simplifications will not affect the main conclusions.

The model identifies the following markets – although sometimes the identification is implicit rather than explicit:

1. Spot exchange ⎫
2. Forward exchange ⎪
3. Bonds ⎬ Financial
4. Money ⎭
5. Domestic output ⎫
6. Exportables ⎪
7. Imports ⎬ Real
8. Labor ⎭

In any general equilibrium model there is a redundant market by Walras' Law and on this basis the market for bonds is excluded.

The generic model is intended to be static in the sense that all the relationships are assumed to be instantaneous, i.e. there are no lags. The analysis is therefore essentially long-run. In practice most of the central relationships will tend to be dynamic, in which case our conclusions would only refer to the asymptotic properties of models that incorporated the set of desirable characteristics. Nevertheless, because of stock-flow phenomena even the static model features unavoidable dynamic properties.

A further simplification is the assumption that expectations are predetermined. The generic model incorporates two very important random variables, the expected rate of inflation and the expected exchange rate. These simplifications are substantive to the dynamic properties of the model but not to its static behaviour. However, we return to the endogenisation of expectations in the next chapter.

Finally, the analysis is conducted from the point of view of a small country whose financial and economic behaviour cannot significantly influence world financial and economic conditions. Therefore, overseas interest rates, prices, etc., are taken to be exogenous.

The various aspects of the generic model are discussed in turn. The balance of payments is defined as the sum of the current (CA) and capital accounts (CAP):

$$\dot{R} = CA + CAP \tag{3.1}$$

where $\dot{R}$ ($\dot{}$ denotes the derivative with respect to time) is the change in reserves. $\dot{R}$ is also the excess demand for domestic currency in terms of foreign exchange. For example if $\dot{R}$ is constrained to zero, as would be the case when the exchange rate is floating, an *ex ante* excess demand for spot exchange would cause the spot rate to adjust via equation 3.1. Alternatively, if the exchange rate is fixed, $\dot{R}$ would be the net official supply of spot exchange on the market. Therefore, the balance of payments identity is also the market clearing equation for spot exchange in terms of domestic currency. This equation is based on equation 2.1.

Our approach is to identify all the contingent market forces that may be expected to influence the balance of payments in the generic model with respect to its components. We begin by examining the capital account.

The Balance of Payments

In the generic model the forward exchange market and the domestic and international financial markets are contingent on the capital account. In what follows, we operate with respect to a single domestic interest rate (r) which typically is represented by a short-term interest rate and an overseas interest rate (r_w) of comparable maturity etc. The forward rate (F) is of the same maturity as the interest rate to which it refers. Since we intend to deal with only one financial asset (apart from money) the capital account of the balance of payments becomes synonymous with short-term capital flows as discussed in the previous chapter. Subsequently, drawing on equation 2.20 we may express the determination of the capital account as:

$$CAP = c_1(\dot{r} - \dot{r}_w - \dot{S} + \dot{S}^e) + c_2 \dot{G} \tag{3.2}$$

$$
\left.
\begin{aligned}
c_1 &= \frac{\alpha\beta}{\alpha + \beta} + \gamma \qquad &\text{(i)} \\
c_2 &= \frac{\alpha}{\alpha + \beta} \qquad &\text{(ii)}
\end{aligned}
\right\} \tag{3.3}
$$

In this formulation, first-differences become time-derivatives, and apart from some obvious and minor modifications in notation equations 3.2 and 2.20 are essentially the same. $\dot{G}$, $\dot{S}^e$ and $\dot{r}_w$ are assumed to be exogenous. $\dot{S}$ will be zero if the exchange rate is fixed. Since a discussion of the capital account in its relationship with the spot and forward exchange markets has already been presented in the previous chapter we turn directly to the specification of the current account of the balance of payments.

The current account is defined as:

$$CA = X \cdot P_x - M \cdot P_w / S \tag{3.4}$$

i.e. the difference between export values and import values where:

X = volume of exports
P_x = export prices expressed in domestic currency
M = import volumes
P_w = world price expressed in foreign currency

Unfortunately this expression is non-linear whereas a linear model is required for analysis. Therefore we approximate the current account identity as:

$$CA \simeq X + P_x - M - P_w + S \tag{3.5}$$

i.e. as if the variables were logarithms and the current account were expressed as the ratio of export values to import values. Also there is an implicit linear relationship between the spot rate as conceived in this equation and as it was conceived in the previous chapter.

Equation 2.2, the determinants of the supply of exportables, may be linearised (ignoring constant terms) as:

$$XS = a_1(P_x - P) \tag{3.6}$$

where P is the price of non-traded domestic output, i.e. the supply of exportables varies directly with the relative profitability between the production of exportables and the production of domestic output in general. For our present purposes we assume that productive potential is fixed and we continue with the assumption made in the previous chapter that relative profitability does not depend on costs. However, these assumptions do not affect the conclusions.

Equation 2.3, the overseas demand for exportables, may be linearised as:

$$X = u_1(P_x - S - P_w) + u_2 WT \tag{3.7}$$

where WT is an index of world trade and u_1 is the familiar price elasticity of demand for exports.

The domestic demand for exportables, equation 2.4, may be linearised as:

$$XD = a_2(P - P_x) \tag{3.8}$$

In equilibrium the supply and demand for exportables must be equal. Since here X, XD and XS are essentially logarithms we must approximate equation 2.6 as:

$$XS = wX + (1 - w)XD \qquad (0 \lessgtr w \lessgtr 1) \tag{3.9}$$

Substituting for XS, X and XD from the previous three expressions implies that export prices are a weighted average of domestic and overseas prices when expressed in domestic currency:

$$P_x = e_1 P + (1 - e_1)(P_w - S) + e_2 WT \tag{3.10}$$

$$\left. \begin{array}{l} \text{where } e_1 = \dfrac{wa_2 + a_1}{a_1 + a_2 w + u_1(1 - w)} \\[3mm] e_2 = \dfrac{(1 - w)u_2}{a_1 + u_2 w + u_1(1 - w)} \end{array} \right\} \tag{3.11}$$

According to equation 3.10 in the limit the price of exportables may be dominated by domestic prices if $e_1 = 1$ and by overseas prices if $e_1 = 0$.

An elaboration of the issues that are entailed here may be found in Beenstock and Minford [1976, p. 88].

Finally, the volume of imports is related to the relative price between domestic and overseas output expressed in domestic currency and on the level of domestic economic activity as measured by aggregate output (Y):

$$M = u_3(P - P_w + S) + u_4 Y \qquad (3.12)$$

In other words, the imports are assumed to be determined by income-expenditure as well as relative price effects. Hoarding and absorption phenomena could be introduced at this stage. However, these aspects are introduced indirectly below.

Using equation 3.5, 3.7, 3.10 and 3.12, the current account of the balance of payments may be expressed as:

$$CA = u_5(P_w - S - P) + u_6 WT - u_4 Y \qquad (3.13)$$

$$\left. \begin{array}{l} \text{where } u_5 = e_1(u_1 - 1) + u_3 \\ \qquad u_6 = u_2 + e_2(1 - u_1) \end{array} \right\} \qquad (3.14)$$

When all the price elasticities contingent on the current account are taken into consideration the Marshall-Lerner conditions will be fulfilled when u_5 is positive. However, these are only the short-run conditions for a devaluation to improve the current account. In the longer term, these conditions would be complicated by further feedback effects regarding the real and monetary sectors of the domestic economy as shall be seen.

Notice that when equations 3.2 and 3.13 are combined into equation 3.1 and the exchange rate is assumed to float (i.e. $\dot{R} = 0$) a first-order differential equation in the spot rate is implied. This arises because the current account depends on the level of the exchange rate whereas the capital account (for given wealth) depends on the stock adjustment process generated by changes in the exchange rate. However, under two-tier exchange rate systems where there is one exchange rate for commercial transactions on the current account and a separate exchange rate for financial transactions on the capital account this dynamic aspect of the model would be eliminated. (Further discussions of two-tier exchange rate systems may be found in Argy and Porter [1972] and Beenstock [1976, pp. 140-4].)

The Domestic Economy – Real

Aggregate output (Y) is made up of domestic output and traded output. Therefore, we have the conventional national income identity that output is equal to domestic demand (DD) plus the foreign resource balance:

$$Y = DD + X - M \tag{3.15}$$

In this generic model the theory of the determination of domestic demand is suitably eclectic in that it incorporates respectively interest rates effects, real balance effects and income-expenditure effects:

$$DD = -f_1(r - x) + f_2(L - P) + f_3 Y \qquad (0 \lessgtr f_3 \lessgtr 1) \tag{3.16}$$

where L denotes the stock of nominal money balances and x the expected rate of inflation, taken here to be predetermined. Equation 3.16 is crucial to the monetary analysis for without it the real and monetary sectors would be dichotomised.

An augmented Phillips Curve is postulated for the labour market:

$$\dot{W} = \upsilon(Y - \overline{Y}) + x \tag{3.17}$$

where since $\overline{Y}$ denotes capacity output, $Y - \overline{Y}$ is a measure of the pressure of demand.

The domestic price level may also respond to the pressure of demand and cost inflation. These costs are made up of wage costs and import costs:

$$\dot{P} = g_1(Y - \overline{Y}) + g_2 \dot{W} + g_3(\dot{P}_w - \dot{S}) \tag{3.18}$$

Combining these two equations implies that:

$$\dot{P} = n(Y - \overline{Y}) + g_3(\dot{P}_w - \dot{S}) + g_2 x \tag{3.19}$$

where $n = \upsilon g_2 + g_1$

The Domestic Economy – Financial

In this simplified generic model we abstract from the banking sector. The money supply is therefore made up of high-powered money alone which originates from two sources, the overseas sector and the domestic monetary authorities. Therefore the change in the money supply is defined as:

$$\dot{L}^s = \dot{R} + DCE \tag{3.20}$$

where DCE denotes the domestic credit expansion of the authorities.

The demand for money is assumed to depend on prices, economic activity and interest rates:

$$L^D = h_1 P + h_2 P_x + h_3 Y - h_4 r \tag{3.21}$$

where if the demand for money is homogeneous to degree one in prices:
$$h_1 + h_2 = 1 \tag{3.22}$$

In equilibrium the demand and supply for money must be equal:

$$L^D = L^S \tag{3.23}$$

These equations close the system since the market for bonds is excluded by Walras' Law.

Integrating the Model

In this section the various stands of the model that have been described are assembled. Equations 3.1, 3.15, 3.19 and 3.23 are represented in the following system:

$$\begin{bmatrix} 1 & u_4 & u_5 & -c_1 D \\ 0 & -\beta_1 & -\beta_2 & -\delta_3 \\ 0 & -n & D & 0 \\ 1 & -h_3 D & -\delta_1 D & h_4 D \end{bmatrix} \begin{bmatrix} \dot{R} \\ Y \\ P \\ r \end{bmatrix} = \begin{bmatrix} u_5(P_w - S) + u_6 WT \\ -c_1(\dot{r}_w - \dot{S} + \dot{S}^e) + c_2 \dot{G} \\ -\beta_3(P_w - S) - f_1 x \\ -(u_2 - u_1 e_2) WT \\ -n\overline{Y} + g_3(\dot{P}_w - \dot{S}) \\ + g_2 x \\ -DCE + \delta_2(\dot{P}_w - \dot{S}) \\ + h_2 e_2 \dot{W}T \end{bmatrix} \tag{3.24}$$

where
$$\begin{aligned} \beta_1 &= 1 + u_4 - f_2 h_3 - f_3 & \text{i} \\ \beta_2 &= u_1 e_1 + u_3 + f_2(1 - h_1 - h_2 e_1) & \text{ii} \\ \beta_3 &= u_1 e_1 + u_3 + f_2 h_2(1 - e_1) & \text{iii} \end{aligned} \right\} \tag{3.25}$$

$$\begin{aligned} \delta_1 &= h_1 + h_2 e_1 & \text{iv} \\ \delta_2 &= h_2(1 - e_1) & \text{v} \\ \delta_3 &= f_1 + f_2 h_4 & \text{vi} \end{aligned} \right\} \tag{3.35}$$

and where D is the differential operator d/dt.

Equations 3.24 are applicable when the spot rate is fixed, i.e. when R is variable. When the spot rate is assumed to float the system becomes:

$$\begin{bmatrix} (u_5 + c_1 D) & u_4 & u_5 & -c_1 D \\ -\beta_3 & -\beta_1 & -\beta_2 & -\delta_3 \\ g_3 D & n & D & 0 \\ \delta_2 & -h_3 & -\delta_1 & h_4 \end{bmatrix} \begin{bmatrix} S \\ Y \\ P \\ r \end{bmatrix} = \begin{bmatrix} u_5 P_w + u_6 WT \\ -c_1(\dot{r}_w - \dot{S}^e) + c_2 \dot{G} \\ -\beta_3 P_w - f_1 x \\ -(u_2 - u_1 e_2) WT \\ -n\overline{Y} + g_3 \dot{P}_w + g_2 x \\ -DCEA - \overline{R} + \delta_2 P_w \\ + h_2 e_2 WT \end{bmatrix} \tag{3.26}$$

where $DCEA$ and $\overline{R}$ denote the stock of money generated through past DCE and $\dot{R}$. In this case $\dot{R} = 0$ and S is variable.

While the model is static in the sense that none of the relationships are specified with lags, there are unavoidable dynamic elements that arise out of the stock-flow relationships that have been incorporated and the Phillips Curve. For example, when the exchange rate is fixed the stock-flow relationship occurs because the money supply is influenced by flows across the balance of payments. When the exchange rate is flexible the same phenomenon occurs because the market for spot exchange is described by a first order differential equation since the current account depends on the level of the exchange rate whereas the capital account depends on the change of the exchange rate. Subsequently, under either formulation the characteristic equation of the system implies a second order dynamic process.

The determinant in equation 3.24 implies the following characteristic equation:

$$D^2 + \frac{Z_1}{Z_2}D + \frac{Z_3}{Z_2} = 0 \qquad (3.27)$$

where:
$$\left.\begin{array}{ll} Z_1 = -(\delta_3 n\delta_1 + h_4 n\beta_2 + c_1\beta_2 n + \delta_3 u_4) & \text{i} \\[4pt] Z_2 = -(\delta_3 h_3 + h_4\beta_1 + c_1\beta_1) & \text{ii} \\[4pt] Z_3 = -\delta_3 u_5 n & \text{iii} \end{array}\right\} \quad (3.28)$$

The system will be stable if $(Z_2 + Z_3)^2 > Z_1^2$ $\qquad$ (3.29)

The determinant in equation 3.26 also implies a second order process:

$$D^2 + \frac{Z_4}{Z_5}D + \frac{Z_6}{Z_5} = 0 \qquad (3.30)$$

where:
$$\left.\begin{array}{l} Z_4 = u_5(\beta_1 h_4 + \delta_3 h_3)(g_3 - 1) \\[2pt] \qquad + (\beta_2 h_4 + \delta_1\delta_3)(nc_1 - g_3 u_4) \\[2pt] \qquad + \beta_3(u_4 h_4 + n\delta_1 c_1) + \delta_2(n\dot{c}_1\beta_2 - u_4\delta_3) \end{array}\right\} \quad \text{i}$$

$$\left.\begin{array}{l} Z_5 = -c_1[\beta_1(\delta_2 + h_4) + h_3(\delta_3 + \beta_3) \\[2pt] \qquad + g_3(\beta_1\delta_1 - h_3\beta_2)] \end{array}\right\} \quad \text{ii} \qquad (3.31)$$

$$Z_6 = nu_5[\delta_3(\delta_1 + \delta_2) + h_4(\beta_2 - \beta_3)] \qquad \text{iii}$$

The stability condition for this system is:

$$(Z_5 + Z_6)^2 > Z_4^2 \qquad (3.32)$$

Our objective here is not, however, to explore the complexity of circumstances under which equations 3.29 and 3.32 would hold. However since the coefficients in equation 3.27 are positive, that system must be stable. A meaningful analysis of stability (as will be argued in the next chapter) entails a wider set of issues than those so far discussed. In particular, it is essential to take account of the effect of expectations on the dynamic structure of the model and so far expectations have been left exogenous. In the meanwhile we proceed on the assumption that there is indeed a stable solution to the two systems and we now turn to a discussion of some of these solutions. We concern ourselves with the long-run responses of the model since the short-term responses are in effect summarised in the structural equations themselves.

Finding the particular integrals of these models requires explicit assumptions about the time-paths of the exogenous variables. For simiplicity we assume that P_w is a constant, in which case $\dot{P}w$ and $\dot{W}T = 0$. By definition $\dot{S}$ is zero in system 3.24, i.e. when the exchange rate is fixed. All the remaining exogenous variables are assumed to be constants. For example $\dot{r}_w$ is the change in world interest rate.

When the exchange rate is fixed the set of particular integrals is:

$$\dot{R} = \frac{nu_5\delta_3}{Z_3}DCE \qquad \text{i}$$

$$P = \frac{n\delta_3}{Z_3}\left[c_1(\dot{r}_w - \dot{S}^e) - c_2\dot{G} - u_5(P_w - S) \right.$$
$$\left. - u_6WT - DCE + u_4\overline{Y} - \frac{g_2u_4x}{n} \right] \qquad \text{ii} \qquad (3.33)$$

$$Y = \frac{n\delta_3 u_5}{Z_3}\overline{Y} \qquad \text{iii}$$

When the exchange rate is flexible the following set of particular integrals is implied:

$$S = \frac{1}{Z_6}\big[(\delta_3 nu_5(\delta_1 + \delta_2) + h_4(\beta_2 - \beta_3))\big]P_w$$
$$+ n\big[u_4(\beta_2 h_4 + \delta_1\delta_3) - \beta_1 u_5 h_4 - h_3 u_5 \delta_3\big]\overline{Y}$$
$$+ n(u_6(\beta_2 h_4 + \delta_3\delta_1) + (u_1 e_2 - u_2)u_5 h_4$$
$$+ h_2 e_2 u_5 \delta_3)WT + n(\beta_2 h_4 + \delta_3 \delta_1)(c_1\dot{S}^e$$
$$+ c_2\dot{G} - c_1\dot{r}_w) + g_2(u_5(\beta_1 h_4 + h_3\delta_3)$$
$$- \frac{nf_1 u_5 h_4}{g_2} - u_4(\beta_2 h_4 + \delta_1\delta_3))x$$
$$- nu_5\delta_3(DCEA + \overline{R})\big] \qquad (3.34)$$

$$P = \frac{1}{Z_6}\Big[-n(u_5(h_4(u_1 e_2 - u_2) + \delta_3 h_2 e_2)$$

$$+ \beta_3 u_6 h_4 - \delta_2 u_6 \delta_3) \, WT$$

$$- u_5 \delta_3 - n(\beta_3 h_4 - \delta_2 \delta_3)(c_1 \dot{S}^e + c_2 \dot{G} - c_1 \dot{r}_w)$$

$$+ g_2 \frac{(n u_5 h_4 f_1)}{g_2} - u_5 \delta_3 (\beta_1 h_4 - h_3)$$

$$+ \beta_3 u_4 h_4 - \delta_2 u_4 \delta_3) x + (\beta_3 u_4 h_4$$

$$- u_5(\beta_1 h_4 + h_3 \delta_3) - \delta_2 u_4 \delta_3) \, \overline{Y}$$

$$+ u_5 n \delta_3 (DCEA + \overline{R})\Big]$$

$$Y = \frac{1}{Z_6}\big[n u_5(\delta_3(\delta_1 + \delta_2) + h_4(\beta_2 - \beta_3))\big]$$

ii

iii

Notice that when equation 3.22 holds $\beta_2 = \beta_3$ and $\delta_1 + \delta_2 = 1$, in which case:

$$Z_6 = n u_5 \delta_3 = -Z_3 \qquad (3.35)$$

Discussion

Formidable as some of these analytical results might first appear, some of the main logical deductions may sound surprisingly simple to some, at the same time as being fairly obvious to others. We shall discuss each of equations 3.33 and 3.34 in turn.

Remembering that $Z_3 = \delta_3 u_5 n$ from equation 3.28 iii, equation 3.33 i states that in the long run the flow of reserves or the balance of payments is equal and opposite to domestic credit expansion. Furthermore, the balance of payments depends on nothing else. If the authorities create money, they must expect that this will eventually be reflected in a balance of payments deficit of the same amount. In other words in this essentially static model where all parameters are assumed to remain unchanged the balance of payments is seen to be a monetary phenomenon as discussed by Johnson [1958], and [1972] in 'The Monetary Approach to Balance of Payments Theory'. This is true even in structures where elasticities of substitution in international trade and payments are finite. The stock-flow logic of the monetary analysis dominates all other considerations such as the income-expenditure linkages in the long run.

Notice that the balance of payments in the long term is insensitive to world economic activity (WT) which obviously may influence the current account in the short term. As world economic activity rises and the demand for exports increases, the pressure of demand builds up in a way that offsets any favourable balance of payments effects. As a monetary phenomenon the balance of payments cannot respond to increases in real demand overseas.

Similarly, the balance of payments in the long term is insensitive to discrete exchange rate changes. A depreciation in the exchange rate may initially generate improvements in the current account (when abstracting from J-curve effects). However, the subsequent expansion of the money supply would trigger inflationary real balance effects which would push domestic prices in an upward direction, eventually offsetting the exchange rate change.

This phenomenon is shown in equation 3.33 ii, where the domestic price level in the long run varies inversely with the exchange rate, and since export prices are a weighted average of domestic and world prices expressed in domestic currency — as in equation 3.10 — a 10 per cent devaluation would lead to a 10 per cent increase in export prices as well as a 10 per cent increase in nominal wages. Thus devaluations cannot influence the balance of payments in the long run; only domestic credit policies can.

When the exchange rate is fixed the domestic price level is dominated by the overseas price level. This is true even if there is not perfect arbitrage in traded goods, a factor often overlooked — e.g. Ball, Burns and Laury [1977, p. 2]. The 'law of one price' need not hold at a structural level but the stock-flow phenomena implied by the underlying monetary processes ensure that it holds in the reduced form. Thus even goods that are not directly traded will be affected as long as at least some goods are traded.

Therefore, when the exchange rate is fixed 'small countries' have no choice but to accept the world rate of inflation in the long run. It follows from this that in the long run and in an open economy trade unions cannot be responsible for inflation because they cannot create it. They can, however, create unemployment in the short term. This will be recognised as another proposition of the 'monetarists'.

However, notice that in equation 3.33 ii the price level does not only depend on world prices. For example if DCE increases the domestic price level increases. The same occurs when $\dot{G}$ rises. This arises on account of the implicit lags generated by the stock-flow framework. If say DCE is raised by 100 into perpetuity, the balance of payments will eventually deteriorate by 100. Before that time, however, the stock of money in the system will build up and the price level will have to adjust upwards via the real balance effect. The longer the lags, the greater is the scope for a price level that is independent of the world price in the long term. In these respects the results differ from the familiar 'monetarist' propositions.

If real output rises ($\overline{Y}$) the demand for money will rise and negative real balance effects will be generated. Subsequently, the price level will fall and during the adjustment process the balance of payments will tend to improve both on the current and capital accounts.

Equation 3.33iii states that in the long run full employment will be achieved. This behaviour is implied by equation 3.17 where real wages are assumed to adjust to eliminate excess demand in the labour market. Alternatively, the 'natural' rate of unemployment will be established as in Friedman [1968].

Equations 3.33 imply that when the exchange rate is fixed the monetary authorities are ultimately responsible for the health of the balance of payments, that the price level or the rate of inflation is largely dependent upon overseas prices and that the economy will have a tendency towards full employment in the steady state. The issues in political economy that arise out of these deductions will be reserved for Chapter 5.

We now turn to the situation where the exchange rate is allowed to float freely. In equation 3.34 i we have the long run determinants of the spot rate. Recalling equation 3.35, we may deduce that the spot rate will vary inversely with the quantity of the money that the authorities create (DCEA); a 10 per cent increase in the money supply through domestic credit policies will eventually generate a 10 per cent depreciation of the exchange rate. Just as with equations 3.33 the balance of payments was essentially a monetary phenomenon when the exchange rate is fixed, the exchange rate emerges as a monetary phenomenon when the exchange rate is allowed to float. However, if equation 3.22 does not hold, equation 3.35 will not hold either and a 1 per cent change in the money stock would not be necessarily associated with 1 per cent change in the exchange rate. In other words, if the demand for money is not homogeneous to degree one in prices, money in these respects will not be neutral as may well be expected.

Equation 3.34 i also implies that if overseas prices rise by 10 per cent the exchange rate will appreciate by 10 per cent, recalling equation 3.31 iii. This is the analogue under flexible exchange rates of the relationship between domestic and world prices in equation 3.33 ii. In other words, the terms of trade are given since $P - P_w + S$ is always constant regardless of the exchange rate regime. This is true even if equation 3.22 does not hold.

Also, notice that as with equation 3.33 ii, the stock-flow logic implies that the exchange rate may depend on world trade, the change in overseas interest rates, etc., i.e. flow variables which influence the level of prices because of the implicit lag in the stock-flow specification, and hence the exchange rate.

Whereas the price level is dominated by overseas factors when the exchange is fixed, equation 3.34 ii indicates that when the exchange rate is flexible it is dominated by domestic monetary considerations and that the exchange rate insulates the domestic economy from overseas forces.

The familiar 'monetarist' proposition that the price level varies proportionately with the money supply in the long run is implied once again when equation 3.22 holds. Also, the price level is affected by flow variables because of the implicit lags in the stock-flow specification.

Finally, equation 3.34 iii is the same as its counterpart in equation 3.33 iii; the economy tends to the 'natural' rate of unemployment when exchange rates are flexible as it does when exchange rates are fixed.

Concluding Remarks

The full policy implications of this discussion as well as its significance for a number of current macro-economic debates are reserved for Chapter 5, since we have yet to consider the all-important matter of the macro-economic role of expectations. In the meanwhile it may be noted that the generic model that has been described has a number of fairly elementary long-run properties. The crucial ingredient of this specification is the assumption, dating back to Wicksell and Hume, that stocks of financial assets are related to flows of expenditures and that the macro-economy is made up of a set of interacting markets. Clearly if these twin assumptions are abandoned, the income-expenditure linkages would emerge as the main analytical feature of the system and macro-economic behaviour would depend on the multiplier-accelerator mechanics which were popular during the 1950s and 1960s. In the present formulation, however, these mechanisms do not have an overriding influence in the long run which is dominated instead by the market stock-flow logic. Nevertheless, short-term behaviour would obviously be dependent on the income-expenditure logic too.

It will be recalled that the generic model was assumed to be linear for expositional purposes. In the further interests of exposition a number of important exogenous variables such as world trade, overseas interest rates, etc., were assumed to have restricted time-forms so that the particular integrals could be easily determined. In practice both these assumptions are likely to be violated and the conclusions so far reached would not strictly obtain. Unfortunately, analytical solutions for non-linear systems are impossible to derive and the same applies to particular integrals when the time form of the exogenous variables is assumed to be unconstrained. Thus while no doubt the above conclusions will tend to hold, aberrations may occur on account of the fact that we are most probably living in a non-linear world, where the time form of exogenous variables is unconstrained. Obviously the size of these aberrations cannot be assessed analytically. However, they may be derived by computer simulation.

Even if we were to continue with our linear format, different time forms for the exogenous variables would increase the number of factors influencing the endogenous variables as well as modifying in certain cases the orders of magnitude of the existing influences. For example, we note that in equation 3.33 i the only factor influencing the balance of payments is *DCE*. However, we assumed that the time-form for world prices (P_w) was a constant. If instead we were to assume that overseas prices are growing over time, this conclusion would alter. For example, if world prices are growing exponentially (i.e. the rate of inflation is constant), world prices would be expressed as:

$$P_w(t) = P_w(o)e^{mt} \tag{3.36}$$

where t denotes time and $P_w(o)$ is the initial world price level. In this case equation 3.33 i becomes:

$$\dot{R} = \frac{nu_5\delta_3}{Z_3}DCE + \frac{AP_w(o)e^{mt}}{Z_2m^2 + Z_1m + Z_3} \tag{3.37}$$

where

$$
\begin{aligned}
A = &-h_3c_1\beta_3m^3 - m^2[h_3\delta_3u_5 + \beta_1h_4u_5 - \beta_3u_4h_4 + \beta_3n\delta_1c_1 \\
&+ g_3m\beta_1\delta_1c_1 - g_3mh_3\beta_2c_1 + \delta_2m\beta_1c_1] \\
&-m[(\beta_2h_4 + \delta_1\delta_3)(nu_5 + g_3mu_4) - g_3m\beta_1u_5h_4 - h_3g_3mu_5\delta_3 \\
&+ \delta_2mu_4\delta_3 - \delta_2mn\beta_2c_1 + \delta_2nu_5\delta_3]
\end{aligned} \tag{3.38}
$$

Clearly there is very little that can be said about that coefficient of $P_w(o)e^{mt}$ in equation 3.37 other than that it is very complicated! Nevertheless, this serves to demonstrate that the time-form of the exogenous variables will affect the long-term solutions.

Related to this is the fact that we have abstracted from considerations of economic growth which as real phenomena could influence the balance of payments. For example, if *DCE* were zero and *GDP* were growing, an excess demand for money would develop which would clear through a surplus on the balance of payments which brought the supply of money to match the demand for money. However, the long-run tendencies that have been identified would be present in growth models too.

4 Expectations

In the preceeding chapters expectations about inflation (x) and the exchange rate (S^e) were assumed to be exogenous. We have already remarked in Chapter 1 (p.1) that the way in which expectations are formed will have an important bearing on a variety of normative issues regarding the formation of policy. Accordingly, the specification of expectations in econometric models deserves particular attention and the practice of specifying some arbitrary proxy for expectations for the sake of completeness is particularly inadequate. However, during the last few years economists have begun to take expectations and their generation more seriously than before e.g. Sargent and Wallace [1975], Barro [1976], in the growing realisation that the rational expectations hypothesis in particular is fairly crucial to the appraisal of intervention policy at both the macro and micro-economic levels.

Apart from expectations about exchange rates and inflation there will in practice be expectations about a variety of different interest rates to consider, expectations about wages, etc., etc. Our purpose here is not to explore in detail the effects on macro-economic behaviour of various hypotheses about these expectations since this would form a study in its own right. Instead we discuss the macro-economic issues that arise from the point of view of an analysis of exchange rate expectations. We choose expectations about the exchange rather than inflation, since our concern in Part B is a number of econometric studies of the foreign exchange market where exchange rate expectations have to be specified. However, in many respects it is possible to make wider economic inferences from an analysis of exchange market behaviour.

Essentially two kinds of hypothesis suggest themselves in the context of expectations formation. Perhaps the most popular has been what is termed here the 'behavioural theory'—where investors and speculators are assumed to adopt an approach to exchange rate forecasting which might be said to imply a rational behaviour on the part of the parties concerned. This somewhat tautological definition of the 'behavioural theory' is as much a criticism of the theory itself as it is of its presentation at this instance. For example, the assumption that speculators extrapolate past movements in the spot rate or, following Modigliani and Sutch [1966], that expectations are a mixture of extrapolative and regressive elements may seem to most of us a reasonable enough way of setting about the difficult and intrepid business of projecting the expected future exchange rate. However, precisely why it would be logical to look at past movements of the exchange rate to forecast its future is not obvious.

Similarly with adaptive expectations as first conceived by Nerlove (1957), where the investor on realising the error of a previous forecast is assumed to adjust his future forecast in the direction implied by the error. For example, if he forecast 100 and the actual was 50, his next forecast would be hypothesised to lie between 100 and 50. However, it is not obvious why he should forecast say 75 if indeed there is new information available that suggests some different expectation.

Extrapolative and adaptive expectations, etc., imply behaviour which is in a sense intuitively acceptable but which possibly, on closer examination, may not be so reasonable after all. If indeed there are reasonable arguments for relating the past to the future then it would be entirely reasonable and rational to look to the past to forecast the future. Indeed it would be reasonable not only to look at past movements n the spot rate but possibly other variables too which are likely to influence the spot rate in the future. This leads us then into the second kind of expectations hypothesis—rational expectations and the associated area of market efficiency.

The rational expectations hypothesis as first conceived by Muth [1961] suggests that the expected exchange rate is the expected value of the exchange rate where this expectation is formed in the light of economic theory and deduction:

$$_tS_{t+k}^e = E_t(S_{t+k}) \tag{4.1}$$

where k is the relevant date in the future. Thus $_tS_{t+k}^e$ is the spot rate expected for time $t + k$ as of time t. The rational theory would therefore suggest the inclusion of variables in the expectations generating function only if economic theory implied that it was rational to do so and the market may be said to be efficient (see Samuelson [1965]) if in forming its expectation about the future it takes into account all available information. Such information would not only include some appropriate deductive model through which the speculator could combine economic variables in a logical way, but it would also include all information on the economic variables which through the model are likely to affect the expected value of the speculative variable.

Whether or not the rational theory is preferable to the behavioural theories is ultimately an empirical matter. It is not intended here to enter into the epistemological question of whether or not economics is of any practical use. Rather it is assumed that it is on an axiomatic basis. However, Walters [1971] suggests that 'consistent' expectations may be preferable to 'rational' expectations since consistency with economic theory is a relative concept whereas rationality may ascribe an absoluteness to economics which many might contest. A useful review of this subject matter may be found in Poole [1976]. However, to an economist the rational theory has the merit of being based on axioms with which he himself is familiar and which he uses to make economic forecasts through the econometric models that he has constructed. A 'black-box' methodology of forecasting the past through some uni-variate autoregressive moving average process is operated by few if any of the major economic forecasting agencies in the world. Rather, the approach has been to think out how the macro-economy works and to test these ideas empirically.

There are a number of private sector agencies that provide forecasts on this basis for which speculators, among others, are customers. Indeed there are agencies that specialise exclusively in foreign exchange rate forecasting. However, since most professional economists do not rely on behavioural methods for forecasting purposes, it seems odd that they should wish to hypothesise that professional speculators, whose liveli-hoods depend upon taking the best possible view, should be so disposed. This does not mean that all rational speculators necessarily operate on the basis of formal forecasts, although such activity would not of course be ruled out. However, it may reasonably be expected that on an informal basis speculators take into consideration the kind of factors to which the formal forecaster might refer.

The Rational Model

According to the rational model the speculator will take account of two sets of information. First, he will consider the likely path of the spot rate in the absence of speculation, i.e. before speculators themselves influence the path of the rate. Equations 3.30 and 3.34 suggest a general solution for the spot rate when the exchange rate is floating. For given assumptions about the exogenous variables in the particular integral, speculators could generate pre-speculative forecasts of the exchange rate, i.e., before they take into consideration their own behaviour on the exchange rate. The general solution of the system implied a second-order dynamic process.

The pre-speculative path of the spot rate is based on the calculation of the spot rate that sets the excess demand for spot exchange to zero. However, it is clear that once speculators have generated their expectations in this way, the post-speculative path of the spot rate, i.e. after speculators have bought and sold on the basis of this calculation, would be different from its pre-speculative counterpart. Therefore, the second set of information that speculators would be unwise to ignore is the likely effect of their own behaviour on the exchange rate. They therefore have to calculate the pre- and post-speculative paths.

In equation 3.26 c_1 was the coefficient on the change in exchange rate expectations and it will be recalled from equation 3.32ii that this coefficient reflected the direct effect of spot speculation and the indirect effects on the spot rate of forward speculation. However, in what follows it is more convenient to use discrete time rather than continuous time as was the case in the previous chapter. Thus, equation 4.1 may be rewritten as:

$$S^e = B^{-1}S \tag{4.2}$$

where B is the backward operator, i.e. $B^i S = S_{t-i}$. By endogenising expectations in this way we would be able to derive the theoretical time-path of the spot rate, which speculators would incorporate into their expectations.

For example, expressing equations 3.26 in discrete time and substituting on the basis of equation 4.2 for $\dot{S}^e$ as:

$$\dot{S}^e = (1-B)B^{-1}S \tag{4.3}$$

the characteristic equation (the analogue of equation 3.30) would become:

$$Z_{10}\lambda^3 + Z_9\lambda^2 + Z_7\lambda + Z_8 = 0 \tag{4.4}$$

where

$$
\left.
\begin{aligned}
Z_9 &= (u_5 + 2c_1)(n\beta_2 h_4 - \beta_1 h_4 + n\delta_1\delta_3 - h_3\delta_3) &\text{i.}\\
&\quad - c_1(h_4\beta_1 + \delta_3 h_3) + \beta_3(u_4 h_4 - nu_5 h_4 + n\delta_1 c_1\\
&\quad - h_3 c_1) + g_2(\beta_1 u_5 h_4 - u_4\beta_2 h_4 - u_4\delta_1\delta_3\\
&\quad - \beta_1\delta_1 c_1 + h_3 u_5\delta_3 + h_3\beta_2 c_1)\\
&\quad - \delta_1(u_4\delta_3 + \beta_1 c_1 - nu_5\delta_3 - n\beta_2 c_1)
\end{aligned}
\right\} \tag{4.5}
$$

$$Z_{10} = -c_1(n\beta_2 h_4 - \beta_1 h_4 + n\delta_1\delta_3 - h_3\delta_3) \qquad\text{ii}$$

$$
\left.
\begin{aligned}
Z_7 &= (u_5 + 2c_1)(h_4\beta_1 + h_3\delta_3)\\
&\quad - c_1(n\beta_2 h_4 - \beta_1 h_4 + n\delta_1\delta_3 - h_3\delta_3) &\text{iii}\\
&\quad + \beta_3(\delta_1 c_1 + 2h_3 c_1) + g_2(\beta_1\delta_1 c_1 - h_3\beta_2 c_1)\\
&\quad - g_2(\beta_1 u_5 h_4\\
&\quad - u_4\beta_2 h_4 - u_4\delta_1\delta_3 - \beta_1\delta_1 c_1 + h_3 u_3\delta_3 + h_3\beta_2 c_1)\\
&\quad + \delta_1(u_4\delta_3 + 2\beta_1 c_1 + n\beta_2 c_1)
\end{aligned}
\right\} \tag{4.5}
$$

$$
\left.
\begin{aligned}
Z_8 &= -c_1(h_4\beta_1 + h_3\delta_3) - \beta_3 h_3 c_1\\
&\quad - g_2(\beta_1\delta_1 c_1 - h_3\beta_3 c_1) - \delta_1\beta_1 c_1 &\text{iv}
\end{aligned}
\right\}
$$

Particular solutions for the endogenous variables would be as in equations 3.34 with the exceptions:

i. S^e is excluded because it has been endogenised.

ii. Dotted variables are replaced as follows:
$$\dot{r}_w = (1 - B)r_w$$

iii. Z_6 is replaced by $Z_7 + Z_8 + Z_9 + Z_{10}$ as we are dealing with difference rather than differential equations.

Clearly, this information is not very useful. In particular, the conditions in 4.5 are at this stage analytically intractable. The stability question, however, is discussed in the next section. Nevertheless, the formulation is illustrative of the 'structural approach' when expectations are assumed to be rationally determined. Likewise, it would have been possible to endogenise expected inflation x in a rational fashion and this would have increased the original dynamic order of the system. However, it is clear that the specification of additional rational expected values does not add to the dynamic order since they all are the same function of B namely B^{-1}

With the exception of the goods market there were no lags in equations 3.26. Lags, however, may be expected in several areas of the model. First, the current account with respect to both imports and exports is unlikely to respond instantaneously to changes in relative prices. Indeed there is a large body of evidence that suggests these lags may extend over several years. For example Hutton and Minford [1975] estimated a 25-quarter lag on price competitiveness with respect to U.K. export demand. Also Beenstock and Minford [1976] have estimated lags of between 4 and 14 quarters with respect to imports and exports for a variety of industrialised countries. Apart from lags induced by slowness in the dissemination of new market information, traders may find that their plans are constrained in the short run, in which case there would be a cost to a sudden change in trading patterns which, with the passing of time and the higher longer-run flexibility of trading plans, would be expected to fall. Short-term capital flows, by contrast, are unlikely to be significantly lagged. The assumption that the short-term capital market is extremely speedy in its responses is borne out by a considerable body of evidence. However, there is evidence of less speedy responses in the case of international long-term capital flows. Apart from the results reported below see Minford [1975, Chapter 4] and Helliwell *et al.* [1971, Chapter *10*]. Another area where lags may be expected to be considerable is in the link between aggregate demand and monetary variables, equation 3.16 and aggregate demand and inflation, equation 3.19. Similarly, the demand for money function is unlikely to be instantaneous (see Price, [1972]).

The real world, therefore, is likely to be highly dynamic and even in the context of the relatively simplified model examined in Chapter 3, it would not be unreasonable to suppose that the spot rate was determined by a tenth-order (or more) system which if stable implied that the long run was nearly always a long way off. However, long lags of this sort are extremely useful to the speculator, who may take advantage of past information to make forecasts of the future. The longer the lags, the more information the speculator has in arriving at his views about the future. As we shall see, such lags provide a useful basis for an econometric specification of expectations. However, where speculators use this information, *ex post* lags will tend to shorten and in the limit they may disappear.

Rational Expectations and Exchange Rate Stability

So far we have outlined the rational model and we have evaded the all-important issue of exchange rate stability. The main reason for this evasion has been that analyses of stability on the basis of linear models can often generate misleading conclusions. On the other hand stability analyses in the context of more plausible non-linear models are not amenable to analytical derivation and would have to be performed using numerical methods.

The implausibility of the linearity assumption is based on the argument that elasticities and market responses are likely to vary directly with the prices to which they refer. Consider, for example, analyses of exchange rate stability e.g. Britton [1970]. If the exchange rate were unstable it would imply that as the exchange rate fell to extremely low levels and the relative price of domestic to overseas output meant that in foreign currency terms domestic output was virtually becoming a free good, the domestic market did not become swamped by overseas demand. The constant elasticity assumption may be useful for analysing local stability inside which responses may be proximated in a linear fashion. However, analyses of global stability cannot reliably be made under the linearity assumption.

In what follows, the rational model and the stability issue are illustrated in the simplest possible case and where the underlying model is assumed, for the sake of tractability, to be linear. However, we shall draw on the argument that for large relative price movements responses are unlikely to be linear in the evaluation of roots. We begin by writing the first of equations 3.26 in discrete time format and on the assumption that exchange rate expectations are rationally determined:

$$[-(u_5 + 2c_1) + c_1 B^{-1} + c_1 B]S = 0 \qquad (4.6)$$

where it will be recalled that u_5 has a negative sign because a rise in the spot rate causes the current account to deteriorate. Similarly a change in the spot rate would generate short-term capital outflows in which case $2c_1 S$ has a negative sign while $c_1(B + B^{-1})$ has a positive sign because

54 The Balance of Payments

an expected appreciation generates short-term capital inflows. Equation 4.6 implies that all other variables are exogenous and that the spot rate (and the forward rate) are the only endogenous variables. The characteristic equation with respect to 4.6 is:

$$c_1 \lambda^2 - (u_5 + 2c_1)\lambda + c_1 = 0 \tag{4.7}$$

where the roots are:

$$\frac{u_5 + 2c_1 \pm \sqrt{(u_5 + 2c_1)^2 - 4c_1^2}}{2c_1} \tag{4.8}$$

An inspection of these roots shows that the first root (i.e. where $+\sqrt{}$) is bound to be greater than unity while the second root (λ_2) will have an absolute value that is less than unity. Therefore in this simplest of cases one root will always be stable whereas the other will always be unstable. For higher order systems there is no such clear-cut rule.

Let us assume, however, that one root implies stability whereas the other did not. It is at this juncture that the non-linearity 'clause' may be invoked since movements in the exchange rate would tend to be bounded by higher elasticities outside the range of local stability. In the limit, hopefully before output becomes totally free in terms of foreign currency (in the case of a depreciation) elasticities will become infinite. These non-linearities therefore impose a boundary condition on the solution which would lead to the exclusion of the unstable root, since its arbitrary constant as implied by the boundary condition would be zero. Or as Muth [1961, p. 326] puts it, 'For a bounded solution the coefficient of the larger root vanishes, the initial condition is then fitted to the coefficient of the smaller root.' If λ_2 is the stable root the expected path of the spot rate measured as a deviation from its equilibrium value $(\bar{S})$ would be

$$S_t^e - \bar{S} = (S_0 - \bar{S})\lambda_2^t \tag{4.9}$$

where S_0 is the initial value of the spot rate. Equation 4.9 implies that the expected spot rate will depend on the spot rate in the previous period:

$$_tS_{t+1}^e - \bar{S} = \lambda_2(S_t - \bar{S}) \tag{4.10}$$

We have so far been assuming that apart from the variables on the right-hand side of equations 3.26 being exogenous, domestic output, prices and interest rates were assumed to be given. In principle this is unlikely, as has been argued in Chapter 3. Indeed, we have already shown that endogenising these variables implies three roots in equation 4.4. If, for example, two of these were unstable, the non-linearity 'clause' could be invoked to eliminate them and the stable root would dominate. Similarly, when lags generate additional roots the non-linearity 'clause' may be applied once again to eliminate any unstable ones.

The economic interpretation of the non-linearity 'clause' would be that speculators, in being rational, realise that the bottom cannot fall out of the foreign exchange market and therefore ignore any arguments that suggest that it would do so. This is analogous to the argument that if speculators expect an exchange rate to apply at some future date they will base their interim expectations on this long-run expectation. Technically speaking, the boundary condition implied by the long-term view would constrain the solution path for expectations. The rational speculator would not therefore be so unwise as to make one-period-ahead forecasts. In a sense, therefore, he has to generate a forecast functional, i.e. the entire forecast trajectory in one operation.

Uncertainty and the Pattern of Exchange Rate Movements

The theory of rational speculation does not imply that speculators enjoy perfect certainty. On the contrary, the theory explicitly takes uncertainty into account. If indeed the expected variance on the rational expectation were zero, there would be no risk attached to speculation and portfolio theory would suggest that all speculation schedules would be infinitely elastic. Any expectation would be acted upon until the current price was driven into line with the expected price. If, more typically, expected variances are non-zero, speculative elasticities would become finite–speculators are not prepared to back their forecasts to the hilt because they are assumed to be averse to risk. Recalling the definition for c_1 from equation 3.3 we are reminded that the parameters β and γ, the slopes of forward and spot market speculation schedules, will be the only ones to be affected by considerations of exchange rate uncertainty and risk aversion. β and γ would approach infinity as risk was eliminated, and in this limit equation 3.3i would become:

$$c_1 = \alpha + \infty \tag{4.11}$$

Under these circumstances equation (4.7) may be rewritten as:

$$\lambda^2 - 2\lambda + 1 = 0 \tag{4.12}$$

which factorises as $(\lambda - 1)^2$. Therefore, the roots are unity and equation 4.10 becomes:

$$_tS^e_{t+1} = S_t \tag{4.13}$$

i.e. the expected spot rate is equal to the current spot rate. In practice $_tS^e_{t+1}$ will be a random variable in which case equation 4.13 will recognised as the familiar random walk hypothesis about efficient markets (see e.g. Fama [1970]).

If equation 4.13 is substituted into equation 4.6, i.e. if we assume a situation of perfect certainty regarding exchange rate expectations, equation 4.6 becomes $-u_5 S = 0$ i.e. the exchange rate never deviates from its equilibrium value. In other words, when expectations are assumed to be formed rationally and to be held with perfect certainty, speculative behaviour will make sure that the foreign exchange market is never out of equilibrium. If, however, rational expectations are not held with perfect certainty and subsequent considerations of risk aversion imply that $\lambda_2 < 1$, any deviations from equilibrium will be eliminated over time and the observed disequilibria would reflect the subjective uncertainty and risk aversion of speculators.

In general, recalling equation 4.4 and remembering that in practice structural relationships are likely to be lagged, the characteristic equation for the economy as a whole is likely to be some high order polynomial of the form:

$$c_1 \lambda^J - (u_5 + 2c_1)\lambda^{J-1} + \sum_{j=2}^{J} \lambda^{J-j} = 0 \qquad (4.14)$$

and the expected spot rate will tend to be a function of an entire history of previous movements in the spot rate (as well as a relevant vector of exogenous variables). However, when rational expectations are held with perfect certainty, and we take the limits of equation 4.14 as c_1 tends to infinity, we arrive once more at equation 4.12. And when we substitute equation 4.13 into a more dynamic form of equation 4.6 (for which equation 4.14 is the characteristic equation), we find once again that the expansion becomes $-u_5 S = 0$, implying that the exchange rate is always held in equilibrium by speculative behaviour.

How does this arise? Essentially what happens is that because speculators are assumed to know with certainty all the lag structures of the economy and subsequently (in the absence of unforeseeable random events) believe that they can predict the future with certainty, they do not wait for the future price change to take place. Instead they anticipate in their speculative behaviour what is likely to happen; and the future, as it were, collapses on the present. Since ultimately the exchange rate is *ex hypothesi* expected to return to equilibrium in the long run, it never actually gets out of equilibrium.

Perfectly certain rational expectations are of course a limiting case, but none the less interesting since they illustrate how rational expectations are likely to alter the dynamic structure of economic models. In practice, because of random shocks, this case will never arise and even the most cunning rational speculators will be averse to risk.

It should further be noted that the rational model, under conditions of uncertainty, would not preclude a stable oscillatory path for the exchange rate. Such a possibility would be more likely in higher order systems as represented by equation 4.14. An oscillatory path around the long-run equilibrium level would imply that speculators were content to watch the exchange rate overshoot its equilibrium value. It may be asked—why should they allow this if they are rational? The answer is that they are uncertain about their views. If indeed they were more confident an oscillatory path could be very significantly reduced. Nevertheless, it is their lack of confidence that causes them to let the spot rate lurch past its long-run equilibrium.

This essentially theoretical discussion should be distinguished from the statistical work that has been reported on prices where speculation is important, e.g. Cootner (ed.) [1964] and Labys and Granger [1970]. Much of this statistical work has been concerned with the spectrum of the price series under examination. If the spectrum of first differences (6r some other stationary transformation) is flat it implies that prices cannot be forecast from their own past values and that price movements are entirely random. In the vast majority of these studies no reason has been given why prices should be expected to be autocorrelated in the first place. One can only presume that the underlying idea is the 'chartist' one that from a behavioural point of view speculators look to past prices for inspiration about the future in an *ad hoc* fashion. But precisely why 'chartism' is a sensible hypothesis to test is obscure. Moreover, the statistical randomness of prices has little to do with their economic randomness. Essentially, the economist is for ever asking himself—what is an appropriate random-number generating process where this process is a function of a set of explanatory variables?

The rational model, on the other hand, would imply that prices will tend to be autoregressive in the presence of uncertainty. However, it would also suggest that prices will be influenced by the exogenous variables too. If the spectrum of first differences does not imply a random walk this would not serve as evidence that the market in question was not efficient. On the contrary, it could serve as supporting evidence for the efficient markets hypothesis in the presence of risk aversion and uncertainty, and estimates of these parameters. The flatness, or otherwise of spectra is irrelevant to the question of whether or not speculative markets are efficient.

Econometric Considerations

In Part B the expected spot rate will appear in the various econometric models that are estimated, and it will be necessary to derive estimable expressions for S^e—the expected spot rate. In this section we draw upon the ideas already developed in this chapter in an attempt to suggest the form of such estimable expressions. However, the estimation periods range over times when exchange rates were flexible, e.g. Canada in the 1950s, and when exchange rates were fixed. Indeed, the majority of the estimation periods examined relate to fixed rather than flexible exchange rate regimes.

The previous sections related to flexible exchange rates only. If, however, the authorities are hypothesised to react to exchange rate movements in a stabilising fashion, e.g., they support the exchange rate when it is falling and vice versa, i.e. if

$$(1 - B) R = k(1 - B) S \qquad (4.15)$$

it would be possible to solve the rational model by endogenising the change in reserves in accordance with equation 4.15. The difficulty arises when the authorities peg the exchange rate and only adjust it after a period of time. The rational speculator would therefore have to consider two interrelated factors. First, he would have to calculate the pressures on the spot market along the lines that have already been described. Then, he would have to make an assessment of the likely effects of these pressures on the authorities' foreign exchange market policies. A possible hypothesis about the authorities' behaviour would be that they are prepared to defend the peg up to a given reserve loss, in which case the speculator would have to make an assumption about this limit and then calculate the likely path of the reserve loss. It is clear that the complications engendered by adjustable pegs are formidable and the discussion below merely scratches the surface.

The specification of exchange rate expectations when the exchange rate is floating is relatively simple and since this will provide a basis for considering the complexities of the fixed rate case we dispose of it first. In what follows $F(B)$ is a function of the backward operator and therefore denotes a lag structure. The general solution for the spot rate under the assumption of floating was of the form:

$$S_t = F_1(B)S + F_2(B)X + e_t \qquad (4.16)$$

where X represents the vector of exogenous variables such as overseas interest rates and prices, world trade, etc., etc., and where e_t is a random variable. We may regard an equation of this form as a rational predictor of future exchange rate developments. In the absence of separate forecasts of the exogenous variables we may rewrite equation 4.16 as an infinite moving average process,

$$S_{t+1}^e = \sum_{i=0}^{\infty} w_i S_{t-i} + e_t \qquad (4.17)$$

it may be shown that the forecast variance increases with k, the length of the forecast period. The one-step predictor is given by equation 4.17. Predicting k steps ahead may be carried out recursively.

$$S_{t+k}^e = \sum_{i=1}^{k} w_i S_{t+k-i}^e + \sum_{i=k}^{\infty} w_i S_{t+k-i} \qquad (4.18)$$

The mean square error of predicting k periods ahead is:

$$\sigma^2(S^e_{t+k}) = \sigma_e^2 \sum_{i=0}^{k} v_i^2 \qquad (4.19)$$

where σ_e^2 is the variance of e in equation 4.17 and the vs are the coefficients of the moving average representation of equation 4.17:

$$S_t = \sum_{i=0}^{D} v_i e_{t-i} \qquad (4.20)$$

Thus the uncertainty of forecasting the exchange rate increases with k since:

$$\sigma^2(S^e_{t+k+1} - S^e_{t+k}) = \sigma_e^2 v_{k+1}^2 > 0 \qquad (4.21)$$

These observations will be relevant to the empirical work on the term structure of forward rates in Chapter 8 where the elasticity of the speculation schedule would be expected to vary inversely with the maturity under consideration.

Equation 4.16 may be rewritten as:

$$S_t = (1 - F_1(B))^{-1}(F_2(B)X + e_t) \qquad (4.22)$$

in which case the expected spot rate may be proxied by a set of distributed lags on the exogenous variables. This functional form would correspond with the rational expectations model that has been described. However, it would be most unlikely that having completed the econometric model the values of the spot rate implied by the model were not significantly different from those implied by the estimated version of equation 4.22. Discrepancies are obviously attributable to the inevitable statistical simplicity that would be required in order to estimate equation 4.22. This equation should in principle be regarded as a first shot at the reduced form for the exchange rate and a means for starting up what would be a formidable estimation programme. This programme would proceed as follows:

i. Estimate the model using equation 4.22 to replace S^e. This would provide an initial estimate of $c_1(1)$ – the speculative coefficients from the first iteration.

ii. Using $c_1(1)$ and the estimated model, solve for $S^e(1)$ – the expected spot rate that is implied by this initial model.

iii. Re-estimate the entire model (where relevant) substituting $S^e(1)$ for S^e. This is the second iteration.

iv. Having obtained $c_1(2)$ solve for $S^e(2)$ and repeat the process.

v. Iterations continue until $S^e(h)$ and $S^e(h-1)$ are not significantly different.

In the present study, only the first iteration is considered since we do not have a full model of the economy to carry out stage ii. In any event, model builders might be tempted to stop at stage i because of the formidable estimation programme that is involved.

We now turn to the tricky issue of an appropriate modification of equation 4.22 when the exchange rate is fixed but adjustable. In a regime of fixed but adjustable rates the determination of expectations alters radically. While individual views about the expected exchange rate will vary, the adjustable peg system creates a duopolistic situation with the market on the one hand and the authorities on the other. Whereas under flexible rates the speculator faces the single problem of taking views about what the exchange rate is likely to be at some future date, under the adjustable peg system he is confronted by the two-fold question of not only what the equilibrium rate is likely to be, but also when the authorities are likely to adjust the rate. In what follows, the analysis for the floating rate is used to determine what the exchange rate should be but is modified to allow for the problem of predicting when the authorities will adjust the peg.

Thus if the expectation of the spot rate in any period is taken from equation 4.22, under the new scenario the expectation becomes πS^e where π is the probability that the authorities will have adjusted the peg by some relevant future date. Forecasting the timing of parity changes begs the fundamental question about the factors that motivate governments to adopt adjustable pegs rather than flexible rates. Until very recently, of course, the Bretton Woods system required governments to adhere to fixed but adjustable parities, although some countries such as Canada opted out of this general agreement. During the Bretton Woods era therefore governments did not positively choose to adopt adjustable pegs as an on-going objective, although of course a choice was made in 1945. And during this era many countries showed a reluctance to adjust parities even when 'fundamental disequilibria' existed. The factors behind this reluctance are not discussed here. However, it would seem that the timing of parity changes when governments positively elect for adjustable pegs are likely to be determined by different factors than when governments felt obliged to defend existing parities, sometimes at a very high cost, under the Bretton Woods system. In particular, the frequency of parity changes under the former conditions is likely, in practice, to be greater than under the latter conditions.

A possibility explored here is that the authorities look to a vector of 'pressure' variables in determining their exchange rate policies when the peg is adjustable. For example if the exchange rate is undervalued the reserves would tend to accumulate. At first the authorities might not pay too much attention, however, their ability to do so will fall as the accumulation gathers momentum. As it were, events pressurize the authorities into acting upon the exchange rate. The same occurs, except in the opposite direction when the exchange rate is overvalued. At first the authorities can ride the reserve loss, but after a while they are less able to do so.

There can of course be no clear conclusions regarding the determinants of officials exchange rate policy. However, it seems reasonable to incorporate pressure variables into specifications of exchange rate expectations when the peg is adjustable. Obvious contenders are the reserve movements or the current account of the balance of payments.

For example let us assume that over the recent past the balance of payments has been in equilibrium and that domestic prices are in line with world prices. This picture is disturbed by an increase in world prices by 10 per cent. If the exchange were floating equation 3.34 i suggests that the exchange rate would appreciate by 10 per cent. However, if the exchange rate is fixed the current account will begin to improve. Actually at first it may deteriorate since import prices will be higher, but assuming that the Marshall-Lerner conditions are fulfilled the current account will eventually improve. The probability that the authorities will concede the 10 per cent appreciation is assumed here to vary with the accumulation of the current account. In this way the expected exchange rate not only depends on the past history of the underlying rational variables such as the difference between domestic and overseas prices expressed in terms of domestic currency, but also on a moving average of the pressure variables. For example we may write:

$$S^{e} = \sum_{i=0}^{J} w_{i}(P_{w} - S - P)_{t-i} + \sum_{i=0}^{K} v_{i} CA_{t-i} \qquad (4.23)$$

A given deviation from purchasing power parity will imply a greater expected depreciation the greater the recent history of current account deficits. Similarly, a given history of current account deficits will call for a greater expected depreciation the greater the deviation from purchasing power parity. The forms of the distributed lags in equation 4.23 could be much complicated by J-curve effects since in the wake of a devaluation the current account may initially deteriorate. If speculators were to interpret them as signs of balance of payments weakness an element of irrational instability would be introduced. It is therefore necessary to ensure that the interaction between the w^{s} and the v^{s} does not imply such behaviour if expectations are formed rationally.

Concluding Remarks

This chapter has concentrated almost exclusively on some of the implications of the rational expectations hypothesis for the exchange rate and the balance of payments. The reason for this is that the rational expectations hypothesis has an obvious appeal to economists since it assumes that speculators behave as economists might advise them. The motivation here hopefully transcends a misplaced sense of professional vanity since in risking their money it is in speculators' interests to be as right as they can and this entails a rational assessment of the appropriate economic forces.

In the last analysis, of course, what matters is the empirical content of the various hypotheses about expectations regardless of one's logical prejudices. However, it is curious to note that the history of price behaviour has been one of global (if not always local) stability; goods have neither become free nor infinitely expensive as a result of speculative pressures. While this would only be coincidentally implied by the various behavioural approaches, global stability is an integral feature of the rational expectations hypothesis.

Also it is important to distinguish between 'fully-blown' rational expectations (see Laidler [1976, p. 70–7] from the belief that expectations are based realistically on some appropriate set of economic variables. At the level of econometric estimation this milder form of the hypothesis—or quasi-rational expectations—most probably becomes a practical necessity, and one may accept equation 4.23 without necessarily endorsing the full implications of the rational expectations hypothesis.

5 Balance of Payments Policy

In this chapter we draw together some of the main policy implications of the discussion so far. It should of course be recalled that as yet no empirical estimates have been provided and that the discussion has been theoretical. Nevertheless, a number of interesting theoretical conclusions may be reached regarding macro-economic policy in general and the balance of payments in particular.

Indeed, an essentially theoretical analysis may have certain advantages over the empirical approach of econometric modelling. During the last two decades in particular econometric models have become increasingly important not only within academic circles but also as aids to policy analysis for governments, and there are now a considerable number of private companies that supply econometric services on a commercial basis. However, despite this expanding body of experience econometric modelling continues to be a hazardous endeavour for a variety of reasons that relate to our inability to execute controlled experiments with the economy. Thus despite the numerous methods for treating simultaneity and estimating distributed lags it is still very difficult to isolate the influences of cause and effect on parameter estimates and satisfactorily to identify distributed lags. The latter becomes especially difficult when there are several explanatory variables that are dynamic and this compounds the difficulties of distinguishing between the serial correlation of the errors and the dynamic structure of the model itself. In addition to this are the problems imposed by multicollinearity and the absence of observations regarding many crucial variables such as expected inflation.

Our purpose here is not to list and discuss the major estimation difficulties, but to remind ourselves how fragile and potentially misleading many of our more ambitious econometric constructs may be. In addition, it is often the case that econometric models are incomplete in the sense that a sector or a market is not included for one reason or another. For example for many years the model used by the U.K. Treasury (see H.M. Treasury [1975]) has not had a monetary sector and the result in these cases is often like 'Hamlet without the prince'. It is probably no coincidence that in the U.K. the authorities attached such a disproportionately low priority to monetary policy during this decade; the absence of an econometric facility in the monetary sector was most probably responsible in part for a set of policies that were conceived almost as if money did not exist or matter since the model did not 'say' that it did exist or matter.

Thus in the light of the numerous pitfalls and shortcomings that are inherent in econometric modelling the theoretical approach at least has the advantage of setting out where the logic of many models would lead, and it is most probably the case that the structure of the model that has been discussed in Chapters 2 and 3 will be acceptable as a basis to many econometric model builders. This of course does not detract in any way from the importance of applied econometric investigation (as is endorsed by Part B) and its role in testing out various hypotheses.

We begin by recalling some of the issues in the debate about 'monetarism'. Thereafter, we discuss the complications that are implied by the analysis regarding the policy assignment question. Finally, the case for discretionary macro-economic policies is discussed. While our concern here is largely with the balance of payments and the exchange rate, the opportunity is taken to relate the analysis to other areas of macro-economic policy.

The Analytical Case for Monetarism

In a small open economy with a fixed exchange rate the balance of payments in the long run is equal to the money supply that the authorities create. This indeed is the main conclusion of the Monetary Approach as conceived by Johnson [1972] and others and it implies that the balance of payments will only improve if the monetary authorities stop printing money.

Critics will argue that the truth is not so simple and the exasperated policy maker who has tried every conceivable device for curing the balance of payments deficit may well be understandably incredulous. Nevertheless, equation 3.33i endorses the Monetary Approach even though it has been derived through a fairly sophisticated economic model. How is the credibility gap to be narrowed and under what circumstances is it justifiable?

It must be emphasised once more that these results are asymptotic. At any moment in time, because of lags, increases in domestic credit are unlikely to be reflected in equal and opposite balance of payments deficits. Indeed, in the short term, the 'structural approach' emphasises the complex of economic forces that will influence the balance of payments and it is for this reason that successful short-term balance of payments policies are very difficult if not impossible to implement short of quantitative restrictions on the current and capital accounts of the balance of payments. On the other hand the stable monetary policies that will eventually restore stability to the balance of payments may be beyond the political horizons of the policy maker who, as it were, does not want to be caught out between the lags at election time. The resultant political economy of short-term expediency at best merely postpones the problem and at worst compounds it.

A related source of possible incredulity is the conclusion as in equation 3.33ii that when the exchange rate is fixed a small open economy's price level is dictated by the world price level. This at least passes the blame for domestic inflation on to overseas events and exonerates the trade unions from being responsible for domestic inflation. However, here too it is necessary to distinguish the short term from the long term to which these conclusions refer. For example, say that wage rates have been summarily increased by 10 per cent. In the short run, via equations 3.18 and 3.19 domestic prices would rise. Via equation 3.16 domestic demand would fall and some unemployment would ensue. On the balance of payments, the higher domestic price level would increase export prices via equation 3.10 and the volume of exports would fall while the volume of imports would rise, compounding the fall in GDP. During the second 'round' the fall in GDP would cause a reduction in nominal wages via equation 3.18 and the process would be repeated. Indeed, these 'rounds' will continue until the full increase in nominal wage rates has been reversed and the price level will have been restored to its original level. In other words, unrequited wage increases in the absence of complementary monetary expansions generate short-term inflation and unemployment but no long-term inflation.

When the exchange rate is floating we find in equation 3.34i that the responsibility that the authorities bear regarding the balance of payments when the exchange rate is fixed is transferred to the domestic price level. Since a floating exchange rate insulates the domestic monetary economy from external influences the domestic money supply is the responsibility of the monetary authorities. The logic of the model confirms the basic tenet of monetarism that the price level varies proportionately with the money supply. In addition the economy will tend to full employment. In this context the role of the exchange rate is to restore purchasing power parity. Summary wage increases will have the same effects as discussed in the previous paragraph except that the balance of payment effects will manifest as exchange rate effects. In the short term the exchange rate will fall and unemployment will develop. In the long run, the price level, the exchange rate and the volume of unemployment will be unaltered.

The simple 'monetarist' conclusions might, however, be rejected for at least three possible reasons:

    (i) *The model is wrong*. This argument would have to refer to the logic of the model rather than its parameters, although it has already been remarked that the neutrality of money depends on equation 3.22 being satisfied. If the demand for money is not linearly homogeneous in the price level, a doubling of the quantity of money need not lead to a doubling in the price level. The remaining conclusions, however, hold regardless of the parameter sizes as long as they are not zero. Clearly if nominal wages were exogenous and in the long run involuntary unemployment did not disappear, or if the monetary sector were discarded, the conclusions could not hold. The real balance effect and the Phillips Curve are the sine qua nons of 'monetarism'. However, most model designs would admit to both of these in one form or another.

(ii) *Technicalities.* Here the argument would be that the logical structure of the model is correct but that the basic 'monetarist' conclusions are dominated by other technicalities that arise out of dynamic considerations. Those have already been observed in Chapter 3 e.g. equation 3.37, where the overseas price level was shown to influence the balance of payments as well as domestic credit expansion. In addition the implicit lag in the stock-flow logic of the integrated income-expenditure monetary approach may generate non-neutral effects on the endogenous variables, e.g. world trade in equations 3.33ii and 3.34ii. Furthermore the monetarist conclusions were derived on the assumption of a linear model which at best is only likely to be an approximation to the truth. These and related technicalities will serve to complicate the simple 'monetarist' deductions of the 'structural approach' and the point may be reached where the technical factors dominate the analysis.

(iii) *The Length of the Long Run.* The 'monetarist' conclusions are essentially long-run, which may be in the remote future. If the asymptotic tendencies are weak because of long lags and low coefficients, unemployment, balance of payments difficulties or inflation could persist for many years if not decades. However, this is not so much a criticism as a statement of fact whose implications are discussed in the final section of this chapter. In the meanwhile we merely note that while some econometric models might respond to exogenous shocks over a period of several decades this may be due to the difficulties inherent in estimating distributed lags and appropriately modelling expectations, rather than to do with the real world.

The Assignment Issue Revisited

A theory of macro-economic policy that emerged in the 1950s and 1960s, e.g. Tinbergen [1956], Mundell [1962], [1963], was that the authorities could set themselves various policy objectives such as full employment and balance of payments equilibrium and that, as long as they had a number of independent policy instruments such as fiscal and monetary policies equal to the number of objectives, they could achieve their policy goals. Indeed, this theory was most probably accepted in one form or another by the authorities of many of the major industrial countries and formed the basis for activist macro-economic policies regarding the balance of payments, inflation and unemployment. The political attraction of the theory was clear: the available instruments of economic policy gave the authorities the means to achieve objectives such as full employment and a satisfactory balance of payments, which had obvious political appeal.

No attempt will be made here to assess the practical contribution of the policy assignment theory of macro-economic policy, although the international macro-economic history of the post-war era suggests that in many cases and at many times economies were significantly off target regarding internal and external balance. However, this may merely imply that the practitioners of the theory were at fault rather than the theory itself.

The policy assignment approach assumes that the exchange rate will influence the balance of payments while switching expenditure to the domestic economy. It also assumes that an expansion of monetary policy will raise domestic demand and cause the current account of the balance of payments to deteriorate. A rise in interest rates would reduce domestic demand which would strengthen the current account while the increase in interest rates would directly improve the capital account of the balance of payments. In contrast the 'structural approach' of Chapters 2 and 3 implies that the authorities are impotent with respect to the real part of the macro-economy. For example an exchange rate depreciation neither improves the current account in the long run nor does it switch expenditure; it merely raises domestic prices in proportion to the devaluation. Likewise, monetary policy does not affect aggregate demand; it merely affects the balance of payments when the exchange rate is fixed and the price level and thence the exchange rate when the exchange rate is flexible. In other words, the authorities can only influence the monetary part of the economy in the long run, i.e. the balance of payments when the exchange rate is fixed and the price level when the exchange rate is floating.

In the context of the 'structural approach', therefore, there is little scope for policy assignment except that as the cause of balance of payments imbalances when the exchange rate is fixed and inflation when the exchange rate is flexible, the authorities are obviously in a position to restore a satisfactory balance of payments and price stability if they are sufficiently committed. On the other hand the 'structural approach' suggests that since there will be a tendency to full employment in any case there is no need for an assignment of policy to internal balance. Thus if the authorities pursue responsible monetary policies (fiscal policy does not have an independent long-run effect in the 'structural approach') the balance of payments will take care of itself if the exchange rate is fixed, inflation would be under control when the exchange rate is flexible and full employment or the 'natural' rate of unemployment would be automatically achieved by the economy itself.

The 'structural approach' therefore suggests a less activist role on the part of the authorities than does the policy assignment theory. Instead of being the guardians of full employment, balance of payments equilibrium and price stability, the authorities have to allow the economy to find its own internal equilibrium while the balance of payments and price stability would be acceptable as long as the authorities do not behave irresponsibly.

Just as the policy assignment approach was politically attractive, so the passive and less glamorous policy role that is suggested by this static version of the 'structural approach' is lacking in political appeal. The authorities would understandably be reluctant to accept responsibility for misdemeanour regarding the balance of payments and inflation. Also they would be reluctant to admit that there was nothing they could do about unemployment that was consistent with the balance of payments and price stability. On the other hand events have been putting the policy assignment approach under growing pressure at the same time as confirming some of the deductions of the 'structural approach'. For example in their desire to pursue activist employment policies it has been realised by some authorities that this will put the balance of payments and inflation under pressure. The response has been to control inflation directly by prices and incomes policies and the balance of payments by various quantitative restrictions. While prices and incomes policies of various sorts have been implemented by a considerable number of authorities, they so far have drawn back from following these up with balance of payments controls since this might jeopardise international economic relations. Nevertheless, the political pressures have been very strong regarding the direct control of the balance of payments.

The 'structural approach' suggests that if the authorities wish to pursue activist policies, eventually the underlying economic forces of this approach must be thwarted by various controls. On the other hand it is argued that the controlled economy is incompatible with a free society since it implies arbitrary judgements on the allocation of resources and relative prices. For example, who will decide what constitutes a fair wage or a reasonable import quota, etc., etc? In these respects, the controlled economy would be substantively the same as centrally planned economies and it is most probably for this reason that a number of countries (especially the U.S. since 1972) have decided to abandon several features of the controlled economy in favour of a less activist macro-economic strategy. At least this is one interpretation of some recent macro-economic history when considered in the light of the logic of the 'structural approach'.

Lags and Policy Formulation

The main results of the 'structural approach' that are summarised in equations 3.33 and 3.34 refer to the long run and we have already remarked at various instances that the long run may be quite remote. In other words the automatic achievement of full employment may take several years, assuming some initial disequilibrium. Even if in the static context of the 'structural approach' as discussed in the previous section there is no scope for activist or discretionary policies, it might be asked whether in the dynamic context the authorities can do something to speed up the adjustment process. After all, if we are reasonably confident that full employment will be restored in say seven years' time, why should everybody sit back and wait for it to happen? The same question may be asked about the balance of payments and inflation except in reverse. If the long run is sufficiently remote, the impact of various discretionary strategies on the balance of payments and inflation may be discounted in favour of the short-term benefits of these strategies.

Related to the issues raised by these questions is the interest in the control theoretic approach to macro-economic policy formulation as discussed by Livesey [1971], Pindyck [1973] and others. In many respects this approach is the dynamic analogue of the more familiar policy assignment approach since it takes into consideration that the behavioural relationships may be dynamic. Subsequently, the authorities are unlikely to be able to achieve their macro-economic policy objectives simultaneously since the lags will make this difficult. On the other hand the lagged responses may provide the authorities with extra degrees of freedom since in principle one policy tool could be used to achieve two policy objectives in the unlikely event that the lags were in the appropriate form. In the control theoretic approach the authorities are assumed to attempt to minimise the deviations of the economy from its target course over time. For example the objective functional may take the form:

$$H = \sum_{t=0}^{T} (1+r)^{-t} \sum_{k=1}^{K} a_k (T_k{}^* - T_k)_t^2 \tag{5.1}$$

where T_k is the actual value of the kth target variable and T^* is its desired value, r is a discount rate and t denotes time. In equation 5.1 the authorities are assumed to wish to minimise the discounted value of the loss-functional subject to a dynamic economic model where reduced forms are expressed typically as:

$$T_k = \sum_{j=1}^{J} F_{jk}(B)Z_j \qquad (k = 1, 2, \ldots \ldots K) \qquad (5.2)$$

where $F(B)$ is a distributed lag and Z_j is the jth policy instrument. Thus even if the target variables have dynamic solutions as implied by the 'structural approach', control theory would indicate that in general the authorities could pursue discretionary policies that minimised H to an extent greater than natural economic forces.

Let us assume that Pareto optimality obtains at full employment or the 'natural' rate of unemployment, and zero inflation. In other words (sidetracking the issues raised by the optimality of money holdings and inflation as, e.g., in Friedman [1969], Clower [1970] and Hahn [1971]) we assume that inflation is undesirable. In addition we assume that the long-run terms of trade are optimal in so far as optimal tariffs, etc., prevail (see Johnson [1958]). Therefore any deviations of employment, inflation and the exchange rate from their optimal values will lead to sub-optimal situations. While considerable theoretical work still remains to be done on the welfare effects of macro-economic disequilibrium we assume that the *as* in equation 5.1 are known. At this juncture it is worth nothing that this approach differs from a suggestion that the policy maker should invent his own arbitrary values for the T^*s and the *as* where there might be no relationsip at all with Pareto optimality either at the equilibrium or disequilibrium levels.

But before we may begin to determine whether or not activist policies are consistent with the 'structural approach' in its dynamic setting it is necessary to consider why it is that the economy can ever be out of equilibrium in the first place. In Chapter 4 we have already discussed the proposition (see equation 4.14) that if expectations are assumed to be rational and if they are held with perfect certainty markets will be in permanent (Pareto) equilibrium and all prices and quantities will be optimal. This however was dismissed as being unrealistic since in a stochastic world there can never be perfect certainty, in which case it would obviously be irrational to hold rational expectations with perfect certainty. In general, assuming a world of less than perfect certainty the principles of risk aversion would cause speculative parameters to be finite and the rational expectations hypothesis would imply that disequilibrium will not vanish instanteously and that instead they will disappear over time in a stable fashion.

In other words disequilibrium prices reflect the rational and reasonable principles of risk aversion when expectations are formed rationally. Thus a random shock that pushes, say, the exchange rate out of equilibrium will follow a Pareto-optimal path back to equilibrium if expectations are formulated rationally. If speculators are more risk-averse or their subjective evaluations of risk are greater, it will take longer for the equilibrium to be restored. The interim deviations from equilibrium prices reflects the imputed disutility to risk-taking which must be taken into consideration in the welfare calculus. Thus if the equilibrium exchange rate is say 2 and an exogenous shock pushes the price to 2.1, rational speculators are unlikely to sell instanteously until the price falls to 2 since they cannot be certain that the price will in fact be 2. Therefore on the first 'day' they might push the price down to say 2.05, and on the next 'day' to 2.02, etc., until they eventually eliminate the price disequilibrium completely. In practice, of course, each day will bring new random shocks in which case over time the exchange rate will be in the region of 2 rather than 2 precisely.

Therefore, if expectations are formed rationally disequilibrium prices will be optimal and there will consequently be no further role for activist intervention strategies. The same arguments apply to employment policy; unemployment is the result of uncertainty about the level of equilibrium real wages and the dynamic forces that will eventually restore equilibrium in the labour market.

In general therefore the 'structural approach' removes the conditions for activist or discretionary macro-economic policies that would be optimal when expectations are formed rationally. As it were, the economy is on its own optimal control trajectory. This deduction would apply regardless of lag lengths and if the long run is still too long for political tastes there is little other than stoicism that one can recommend.

If expectations are not formed rationally the economy will not be on an optimal path and so the authorities should be able to design activist policies that will improve economic welfare, e.g., as discussed by Modigliani [1977]. However, the authorities must be confident that they are indeed more rational than the market and that they can use tax revenues to intervene in a way that benefits the taxpayers in whose interest they are supposed to be working. Another condition for policy activism is that even if expectations are formed rationally it may be the case that the authorities have access to information that is not generally available to the public. It may be argued that the remedy here is to inform the market rather than to intervene on its behalf. However, there may be situations where this is not possible. For example, let us assume that the authorities have allowed inflation to get out of hand and that the market is anticipating that inflation will be 30 per cent per year. The authorities, however, have vowed to commit themselves to a monetary growth of 10 per cent per year which implies that in the long run inflation will be about 10 per cent per year too. The authorities may announce this intention but a credibility gap may have arisen which may only be closed after a period of time when the reformed behaviour has been observed. In the meanwhile the economy is likely to be plunged into gloom. By intervening in the wage-price mechanism the authorities may be able to prevent a degree of needless recession. Clearly such policies would require the utmost political integrity.

Floating Exchange Rates

The preceding discussion lends itself to a brief commentary on the debate about floating exchange rates since pegged exchange rates are an extreme form of intervention strategy and managed floating a milder case. It should follow from the preceding discussion that as long as expectations in the foreign exchange market are rational, any foreign exchange intervention would be sub-optimal. As it were, the monetary authorities would be assuming an exchange risk which the market itself did not wish to bear for legitimate reasons that would also apply to the authorities. Subsequently, the condition for clean floating boils down very simply to the rationality of exchange rate expectations.

If exchange rate expectations are not formed rationally the authorities may be able to improve welfare by an intervention policy that maximised the appropriate objective functional with respect to the constraints of the model. The optimal degree of management in the float would depend on the degree of irrationality in the formation of expectations. However, it is unlikely that the optimal exchange intervention strategy would imply pegged exchange rates.

When the authorities intervene in a rational framework the effects could be counter-productive and destabilising. We have already observed (on pp. 55–57) that the elasticity of the speculation schedule will vary inversely with the degree of uncertainty and associated aversion to risk. If the authorities intervene in the foreign exchange market on a random basis, the variance of exchange rate expectations is bound to increase, since apart from the usual array of uncertainties that confront speculators they have to forecast the authorities' behaviour, which is a random variable. This in turn is likely to reduce the elasticity of speculation and subsequently it will take longer for equilibrium to be restored. Thus instead of speeding up the equilibration process, intervention may well have the opposite effect. Indeed some econometric results in the following chapter (pp. 86–87) support this view.

In practice the authorities' intervention behaviour might incorporate systematic as well as random components. However, once rational speculators become aware of the systematic component it will be incorporated into exchange rate expectations (according to the principles discussed in Kydland and Prescott [1977]) and the path of the exchange rate would be different from that intended by the authorities. If indeed the authorities' behaviour is perfectly anticipated, the net effects of the intervention could be zero. For example, if the market knows that the authorities are supporting the currency during a

particular period, the exchange rate is unlikely to rise since speculators
would anticipate that during the following period the exchange rate
would fall again.

Thus if the intervention is perfectly anticipated it is ineffectual, and if
it is not perfectly anticipated it could be destabilising. Either way, when
expectations are formed rationally intervention seems inadvisable.

The Political Economy of Rational Expectations

The sentiments of the previous paragraph are not only applicable to the
foreign exchange market, but are equally applicable to all aspects of
government intervention. This covers intervention in the various real
markets and especially the labour market as well as intervention in the
financial markets. If indeed the lags are too long this approach
emphasises the essentially micro-economic policies that would be
required to improve market efficiency rather than the more familiar
macro-economic policies. Lag lengths in say the labour market might be
affected by labour law or procedures for conducting wage negotiations.
In other words, since parameter values are influenced by institutional
factors in the various markets, changes in institutional parameters could
in principle change the parameters of the model and thence the dynamic
behaviour of the economy. Our objective here, however, is not to
explore these possibilities but merely to point out the micro-economics
of market behaviour that would be required to make the system behave
more efficiently.

If expectations are rational and the 'structural approach' is valid what
are the legitimate macro-economic functions of the authorities? The
logic of the preceding discussions suggests a two-fold strategy:

(i) The exchange rate should be allowed to float freely.
(ii) The authorities should adhere to a monetary rule.

The second strand of the strategy would take the form of a given
percentage increase in the money supply. For example if the demand for
real balances is growing by 3 per cent per year it would be efficient if the
authorities allowed the money supply to grow by 3 per cent per year so
that the supply of real balances would not be met by price deflation.
Price deflation would tend to require a costly loss of output during the
adjustment process, which is quite unnecessary when nominal balances
can be increased almost effortlessly. Also the monetary rule would be
perfectly anticipated and this would minimise the uncertainties in the
formation of macro-economic expectations.

The monetary rule is of course a standard feature of 'monetarist'
policy. However, it only follows when expectations are formed rationally in a dynamic system. In other words, it is possible to accept the
'monetarist' positive economics of the 'structural approach' without

accepting any of the 'monetarist' policy prescriptions. To be a normative and positive 'monetarist' it is necessary to accept the logic of the 'structural approach' as well as the belief that expectations are formed rationally.

The implications of the rational expectations hypothesis for political economy are therefore clear. If policy makers wish (as is understandable) to remain activist at the macro-economic level it will be in their interest to reject the rational expectations hypothesis. On the other hand, an acceptance of the implications of the hypothesis would have the additional benefit of releasing some economists' resources for developing more constructive and socially productive policies elsewhere. However, there are already signs that the neo-Keynesian philosophy of policy activism has come full circle and that the United States, which was the first country to become activist under the New Deal, has been virtually the first country to reject these policies under the Nixon, Ford and Carter administrations. Since 1972 the United States has been experimenting with various monetary guidelines, while the dollar has been floating. At the same time various other industrial countries have been discovering that controls on wages and prices can only be used as short-term policies and are undesirable as long-term policy options. It may be the case that, as the logic of economic events unfolds, other countries will begin to experiment with a withdrawal from activist macro-economic policies.

PART B

STUDIES IN INTER-NATIONAL FINANCIAL TRANSACTIONS

6 Econometric Analyses of Forward Exchange Markets

In this and the following three chapters we concern ourselves with a number of empirical considerations that arise out of the capital account sectors of Part A. In particular we concentrate on the behaviour of the forward exchange market and the determination of capital movements in the balance of payments. This chapter focuses on the determination of forward exchange rates along the theoretical lines that were discussed in Chapter 2 (pp. 23–28). We do not repeat the theoretical analysis here, so the reader is advised to refer to the previous discussion.

The empirical issues that are of interest here are as follows:

(i) *The relative importance of arbitrage and speculation in the determination of the forward exchange rate.* This is the ratio $\alpha/(\alpha + \beta)$ in equation 2.15 which has been the focus of interest by previous researchers in this area, e.g. Stoll [1968], Kesselman [1971] and Hutton [1977]. Spraos [1972] has also shown an interest in this ratio in the belief that the Cambist view (see p. 11) that the arbitrage schedule α is infinitely elastic may be tested by seeing whether the ratio is unity. If the ratio is unity then α must be infinite for non-zero values of β. A difficulty here is that if β is small or if the estimate of the ratio is say 0.95, which happens to be not statistically significantly different from unity, it is difficult to infer that α is a large or infinite number.

From a policy point of view the more obvious interest in the ratio relates to the fact that $\alpha/(\alpha + \beta)$ is the coefficient of the change in the official forward position with regard to the balance of payments, as will be recalled from equation 2.20. If the ratio is unity then all of the official forward support will be reflected by an inflow on the capital account for a given spot rate since the support will be taken up exclusively by covered-interest arbitrage. If the ratio is zero all the support will be absorbed by forward market speculation where there will be no offsetting transactions in the spot market.

Notice that this ratio may be estimated from equation 2.15 even if, as is usually the case, data on the oficial forward position (G) are unavailable. All that this will mean is that a variable is omitted and estimates of the ratio will be less efficient than otherwise.

(ii) *The absolute importance of arbitrage and speculation.* As equation 2.20 implies, to determine the structural effects of interest-rate changes on short-term capital movements it is necessary to evaluate the absolute values of the arbitrage and speculation schedules since the marginal response of the capital account to the uncovered differential is $(\alpha\gamma + \beta\alpha + \beta\gamma)/(\alpha + \beta)$. It would also be necessary to identify γ, the coefficient of the uncovered arbitrage schedule in the spot market as in equation 2.17. This issue is discussed in the next chapter and in the meanwhile we assume γ is zero.

If in this case β were zero, an increase in domestic interest rates would not generate any improvement in the capital account regardless of the size of the elasticity of the covered-interest arbitrage schedule. Thus, if covered assets are perfect substitutes as suggested by the Cambists, i.e. if α is infinity, there would be no covered transactions when uncovered interest rates altered if β were zero. In this case there is no supply of risk bearing in the forward market on the part of speculators and without risk bearing there can be no net covered-interest arbitrage flows. Accordingly, we are concerned with the estimates of both α and β.

(iii) *Exchange rate expectations.* Equation 2.15 indicates the relationship between the forward exchange rate and the expected spot rate. In view of the discussion in Chapter 4 on the formation of expectations we are interested in the generation process of expectations. In particular we are interested in exploring the hypothesis that expectations are formed rationally. Since during the observation periods in most cases exchange rates were pegged, the specification suggested in equation 4.23 is the focus of some attention.

One of the constraints on research into forward market activity is absence of data on forward market transactions. Generally speaking, there are no data at all on the forward market transactions of the private sector (although Black [1973] presents an interesting analysis of some inter-war data), and with the rare exception of the Canadian Exchange Fund Account's transactions there are no published official forward transactions. Indeed, most central banks keep their forward position a closely guarded secret. It is for this reason that we concentrate on what we might be able to infer from the price data rather than the transactions data. However, the Canadian data on the official forward position and the author's access to the U.K. data permitted the estimation of equation 2.15, which is a mixed price/transactions approach. Notice that with this equation the official forward position will econometrically identify the absolute values of the arbitrage and speculation coefficients. If the coefficient on $(r_w - r_d + S)$ is divided by the coefficient on G, the result will be α. Then, having obtained α in this way we may solve for β.

An estimate of α may also be made by studying transactions in the spot market. For example, in equation 2.18 the coefficient on the change in the cost of forward cover will be an estimate of α too. In practice there may be problems in reconciling the estimates of α from the spot and forward markets. However, it is useful to have two independent estimates of the same parameter as a cross-check especially in the light of the debate (e.g., see Officer and Willett [1970]) about this parameter. In particular, if both estimates are similar greater confidence in the parameter estimates would be warranted. At this point, however, it is worth noting that the two approaches have different econometric characteristics.

Effects of Simultaneity

In equation 2.18 any failure adequately to take account of simultaneous equations bias would lead to underestimates of α; for a random increase in STC would cause a fall in the forward rate, establishing a negative covariance between the cost of forward cover and the error term. Indeed, this negative covariance could be strong enough to explain the relatively low estimates that researchers have obtained for spot market estimates of α.

We show that inadequate treatment of simultaneity in equation 2.15 would lead to upward biases to estimates of α. Whereas in the past low estimates of α from equation 2.18 could be dismissed by the 'perfect arbitrage school' on the grounds of simultaneity, the forward market estimates of α cannot be so dimissed because the simultaneity argument is reversed. This of course is a negative advantage. However, we also show that in practice the upward bias is likely to be muted by the covariance structure of the explanatory variables.

We rewrite equation 2.15 in stochastic terms where u is a $TX1$ vector of errors:

$$F = X_1 a + X_2 b + u \tag{6.1}$$

where X_1 is a $TX1$ vector of the suspected endogeneous variables $r_w - r_d + S$ and G. X_2 is a $TX1$ vector of predetermined variables that proxy the expected spot rate. Therefore:

$$a^1 = (a_1 \quad a_2) = \left(\frac{\alpha}{\alpha + \beta} \quad \frac{1}{\alpha + \beta} \right)$$

$$X_1 = (x_{11} \quad x_{12}) = ((r_w - r_d + S) \quad G)$$

$$b = \delta\beta/(\alpha + \beta)$$

where δ relates X_2 to S^e. The least squares estimators of a and b are:

$$\begin{pmatrix} \hat{a} \\ \hat{b} \end{pmatrix} = \begin{pmatrix} (X_1^1 X_1)^{-1} X_1^1 [I - X_2 D^{-1} X_2^1 M] F \\ D^{-1} X_2^1 M F \end{pmatrix}$$

where: $M = I - X_1(X_1^1 X_1)^{-1} X_1^1$
$D = X_2^1 M X_2$

Let us consider the estimate of a first. Because $D^{-1}D = I$ and $MX_1 = 0$ we have:

$$\hat{a} = a + (X_1^1 X_1)^{-1} X_1^1 [I - X_2 D^{-1} X_2^1 M] u$$

If $\underset{T \to \infty}{lim} \dfrac{X_1^1 X_2}{T} = 0$ \hfill (6.2)

i.e., if the suspected endogeneous and exogeneous variables are orthogonal in the limit, then:

$$plim(\hat{a} - a) = lim \left(\frac{X_1^1 X_1}{T} \right)^{-1} plim \frac{X_1^1 u}{T} \qquad (i)$$

$$\text{or } plim\,(\hat{a}_1 - a_1) = \frac{var\, x_{12}\, plim\, x_{11}u - cov\, x_{11}x_{12}\, plim\, x_{12}u}{var\, x_{11} \cdot var\, x_{12} - cov^2\, x_{11}x_{12}} \qquad (ii)$$

$$plim(\hat{a}_2 - a_2) = \frac{var\, x_{11}\, plim\, x_{12}u - cov\, x_{11}x_{12}\, plim\, x_{11}u}{var\, x_{11} \cdot var\, x_{12} - cov^2\, x_{11}x_{12}} \qquad (iii)$$

(6.3)

If the expected endogenous variables are orthogonal, i.e. if $cov\, x_{11} x_{12} = 0$ then these *plims* become:

$$plim(\hat{a}_1 - a_1) = \frac{plim\, x_{11}u}{var\, x_{11}} \qquad (i)$$

$$Plim(\hat{a}_2 - a_2) = \frac{plim\, x_{12}u}{var\, x_{12}} \qquad (ii)$$

(6.4)

Plim $x_{11}u$ is likely to be positive because a random improvement in the forward rate is likely to raise the spot rate and lower domestic interest rates through the capital inflows it would tend to generate. In the context of equation 6.4 this would imply that an inadequate treatment of simultaneity would bias upward the estimated coefficient of a_1. *Plim* $x_{12}u$, however, is likely to be negative since an improvement in the forward rate might lead the authorities to reduce their forward support, in which case an inadequate treatment of simultaneity would bias downward the estimate of a_2.

If estimates of a_1 are likely to be upward-biased and estimates of a_2 are likely to be downward-biased, then indirect estimates of α will be upward-biased. In other words, whereas spot market estimates of α are likely to be biased downwards, their forward market estimates would tend to be biased upwards.

If the suspected endogenous variables are oblique to each other the effects of simultaneity become difficult to ascertain. If anything $cov\, x_{11}\, x_{12}$ is likely to be negative since a strengthening of the spot rate would arguably induce the authorities to reduce their forward position, in which case an inadequate treatment of simultaneity in the contexts of equations 6.3 would tend to be self-correcting. This observation is of obvious comfort, given that simultaneity is extremely difficult to treat adequately.

If the suspected endogenous and exogenous variables are oblique too, the analysis of simultaneity becomes extremely complicated and there seems to be little purpose in thrashing out the various qualitative conditions. If anything $cov\, x_{11}\, S^e$ is likely to be positive, since an increase in the expected spot rate will strengthen the spot rate. Subsequently, $cov\, x_{12}\, S^e$ is likely to be negative. Therefore obliqueness between X_1 and X_2 is likely to compound the effects of simultaneity. We now turn to the estimate of b:

$$\hat{b} = D^{-1}X_2^{1}MF$$
$$= b + D^{-1}X_2^{1}Mu$$
$$= b + D^{-1}X_2^{1}(I - X_1(X_1^{1}X_1)^{-1}X_1^{1})u$$

If condition 6.2 is fulfilled: $plim(\hat{b} - b) = 0$.

But if condition 6.2 is not fulfilled, then estimates of b will become contaminated by any failure adequately to take account of the endogeneity of X_1. The general conclusion therefore is that in a multivariate model where there is likely to be obliqueness between the suspected endogenous and exogeneous variables, an assessment of the effects of simultaneity is exceedingly difficult and the simple bivariate analysis may be positively misleading. It is of course difficult to judge where to draw the line between exogeneity and endogeneity. The approach of Kouri and Porter [1974], for example, is to endogenise domestic interest rates; and Hutton [1977] attaches importance to this too in the case of the U.K. Our assumption is that during the observation period domestic interest rates are not significantly affected by international capital movements. In the longer term this may not be the case; however, this would not be an issue as far as the effects of simultaneous equations bias is concerned.

Data Considerations

Four country studies are reported, for the U.K., Canada, France and West Germany. In this single-maturity investigation, the three-month maturity is assumed to be representative. The data are drawn from different observation periods and in the cases of Germany and France data on the official forward position were not available. Where account has been taken of simultaneous equations bias, an instrumental variables approach has been used. Distributed lags were estimated largely along the lines discussed by Almon [1965] and autoregressive error models were estimated where necessary by the iterative Cochran-Orcutt procedure.

In principle, overseas interest rates (r_w) should be represented by a vector of competing interest rates abroad. In practice, the three-month euro-dollar deposit rate in London (source:*Bank of England Quarterly Bulletin*) was specified as r_w in the cases of the U.K., France and West Germany. In the case of Canada, the three-month U.S. Treasury Bill Rate was specified (source:*Bank of Canada Statistical Summary*) in view of the close financial ties between Canada and the U.S. The specification of the euro-dollar rate is appropriate since it is an internationally traded asset and, as will be shown in Chapter 9, this simplification will still permit, e.g., the forward rate for sterling to be influenced indirectly by German interest rates via their effect on the euro-dollar market.

The Forward Exchange Rate for Sterling 1966–1974

The model is quarterly and all the data in equation 2.15 are averages of end-month observations. The domestic interest rate was represented by the three-month Local Authority deposit rate. These data as well as the spot and forward rates were taken from the *Bank of England Quarterly Bulletin*. The official forward position with the market of the Exchange Equalization Account (EEA) was provided by the Bank of England. While the maturity structure of the EEA's forward position was not ascertained, this is unlikely to be important in view of the likely high degree of substitution between short-term forward maturities.

The following representative equation was estimated:

$$F_t = 56.6 + .947(\hat{S} - UD)_t + ·00049103G_t - \sum_{i=0}^{19} w_i RXP_{t-1}$$
$$\quad (11.16) \qquad\qquad\qquad (2.23)$$
$$+ .001 \sum_{i=1}^{10} u_i VB_{t-1}$$

$$(6.5)$$

	w_i		u_i	
1.	0.184	(0.36)	2.03	(2.8)
2.	0.482·	(0.52)	1.82	(2.8)
3.	0.871	(0.71)	1.62	(2.8)
4.	1.33	(0.90)	1.42	(2.8)
5.	1.84	(1.12)	1.22	(2.8)
6.	2.37	(1.35)	1.01	(2.8)
7.	2.9	(1.59)	0.81	(2.8)
8.	3.41	(1.84)	0.61	(2.8)

9.	3.88	(2.09)	0.41	(2.8)
10.	4.3	(2.34)	0.2	(2.8)
11.	4.62	(2.57)		
12.	4.83	(2.74)	$\sum = 11.17$	
13.	4.92	(2.93)		
14.	4.85	(3.07)	1st Degree Polynomial	
15.	4.61	(3.16)		
16.	4.17	(3.23)		
17.	3.51	(3.28)		
18.	2.61	(3.30)		
19.	1.44	(3.27)		

$\sum = 57.16$

3rd Degree Polynomial
$R^2 = 0.92$ $\qquad \sigma = 1.091 \qquad DW = 1.776$
Observation period: 1966 Q1–1974 Q3

where:
F is the deviation of the sterling-dollar forward rate from parity expressed as an annual percentage; i.e.

$$F = 400\left(\frac{\text{forward rate-parity}}{\text{parity}}\right)$$

S is the deviation of £/$ spot rate on the same basis;

$$S = 400\left(\frac{\text{spot rate-parity}}{\text{parity}}\right)$$

Thus the cost of forward cover as a percentage per annum may be approximated as F-S, since interest rates are expressed in these terms.

G is the EEA's official forward position in millions of U.S. dollars.
RXP is the ratio of U.K. export prices to a weighted average of U.K.

competitors' export prices measured in sterling. (See Hutton and Minford [1975, p.3] for further details.)

VB is the U.K. visible balance in £ millions (source: *Economic Trends*, Central Statistical Office, London).

˄ denotes instrumental variable estimate.
't' values are in parentheses.

The observation period straddles two exchange-rate regimes; since June 1972 sterling has not been kept to a fixed peg. On the other hand since the 'floating' of sterling the quantity of spot market intervention (see the 'balance for official financing' in *Economic Trends*, C.S.O.,

London) has not been different from what it was before June 1972. As it were, the floating of sterling has been tantamount to a widening of the bands around an official exchange-rate objective. Consequently, the fact that the observation period apparently straddles two different exchange rate regimes is less problematic than it might seem. Indeed, the residuals for 1972 Q3–1974 Q3 are not significantly different from their previous values.

The expected spot rate in equation 2.15 is specified in accordance with equation 4.23. In other words the underlying rational expectations variable is the ratio of U.K. to overseas prices (RXP); as this ratio rises the exchange rate is expected to fall. The pressure variable (as described on p. 60) is represented by the visible balance; as the moving average of the visible balance deteriorates, so the authorities are expected to feel inclined to allow the peg to alter or less inclined to support the spot rate.

The equation that is reported is representative of a number of similar estimates. The adjusted uncovered differential ($\hat{S} - UD$) is highly significant and the official forward position is shown to have a significant effect on the forward exchange rate.

The equation suggests that almost 95 per cent of the variance in the forward rate is explained by arbitrage and that $\hat{\alpha} = \$1929\,m$. Both these conclusions are consistent with *a priori* expectations. The equation also implies that almost 95 per cent of official forward sales will be reflected in equal and opposite spot market transactions. The equation further implies that if U.K. interest rates (LA 3-month rate) rise by 1 per cent, while the initial effect would be to attract inflows of $1929 million the final effect would only be $102 million. However, the same increase accompanied by $1827 million official purchases of forward sterling would achieve the full structural inflow. In other words, because the speculative supply of forward cover is relatively inelastic official purchases have an important influence on arbitrage transactions.

The slope of the speculation schedule, β, was estimated at 103, i.e., if the expected spot rate falls below the forward rate in annual terms by 1 per cent, speculators will sell $103 million of forward sterling. This will depress the forward rate and induce spot outflows through covered arbitrage. This evidence suggests that aversion to exchange risk has a considerable dampening influence on forward market speculation.

Since covered-interest arbitrage is almost bound to be less risky than uncovered forward market speculation, one would expect β to be less than α, as indeed the results show. This is contrasted with Hutton's [1977, p. 36–7] seemingly implausible result that β is several times larger than α. At the very least therefore one would expect the ratio $\alpha/(\alpha + \beta)$ to be greater than 0.5. The table summarises estimates of this ratio by other researchers.

THE RATIO OF ARBITRAGE: TOTAL FORWARD MARKET ACTIVITY

Source	$\alpha/(\alpha + \beta)$
Hutton [1977, pp. 36–7]	0.24
Minford [1975, p. 120]	0.493
Argy and Hodjera [1973, p. 50]	0.909
Stoll [1968, p. 67]	0.6366

Our estimate of this ratio is therefore higher by comparison. However, Minford's result is implausibly low and Argy and Hodjera's estimate is biased downwards, since it is based on a regression of the cost of forward cover on the uncovered differential (and is consequently mis-specified). It is interesting to note that while our estimate lends the most support to the Cambist doctrine that the forward rate is dominated by arbitrage and consequently that the ratio should be unity, it does not imply that the arbitrage schedule is infinitely elastic.

The long lag on the relative price term is consistent with lagged adjustments in the current account to RXP. The long-run coefficient, given the confidence intervals, is consistent with the argument that a 1 per cent loss of competitiveness requires in the long run a 1 per cent depreciation to correct it. However, it should be recalled that the lag structure on both RXP and VB (the visible balance) are complex reduced forms.

The Forward Exchange Rate for the Canadian Dollar 1950-1970

The Canadian data were monthly and the observations were as of end-months. Two representative results are reported since the observation period of October 1950 through May 1970 naturally falls into two sub-periods. The first period, upto June 1961, was a period of floating exchange rates, whereas for the remainder of the period the exchange rate was pegged. These results are respectively:

$$F_t = 31 + .794 \underset{(18.24)}{(r_w - r_d + \hat{S})_t} + .00012237 \underset{(5.9)}{G_t} - \sum_{i=0}^{19} w_i RXP_{t-1} \tag{6.6}$$

$$R^2 = 0.988 \, DW = 1.97 \, \sigma = 2.6$$

$$F_t = 12.4 + .9819 \underset{(5.7)}{(r_w - r_d + \hat{S})_t} + .000169 \underset{(3.8)}{G_t} + \sum_{i=1}^{17} v_i S_{t-1} \tag{6.7}$$

$$R^2 = 0.92 \, DW = 1.83 \, \sigma = 2.4$$

where:

F and S are defined as in the case of £. Unless otherwise stated, all data may be found in the *Bank of Canada Statistical Summary*. The Exchange Fund Accounts official forward position (G) is measured in millions of U.S. dollars. The domestic interest rate is the three-month Treasury Bill Rate and the overseas rate is the U.S. Treasury Bill Rate. RXP is conceived as in the case of equation 6.5. Both equations have first-order autoregressive errors (unreported).

Due to difficulties in deriving satisfactory results with regard to the proxies for the expected spot rate only the lag lengths are reported. When the exchange rate was flexible the relative export price proved to be the least unsatisfactory proxy, suggesting that the market expected the spot rate to correct over time for past differentials in inflation rates. Over the fixed rate period the lagged values of the spot rate itself were specified, implying that the market expected the authorities to intervene in the spot market in the light of past behaviour of the spot rate. However, our principal concern at the present time rests with the estimates of $\alpha/(\alpha + \beta)$ and $1/(\alpha + \beta)$.

These estimates implied the following results:

	α	β
Flexible rates	8172	2121
Fixed rates	5803	107

Thus an improvement in the covered differential of one percentage point generates a desired covered-arbitrage inflow of the stock adjustment variety of $8172 million when the spot rate is flexible and $5802 million when it is fixed. These results may be compared with a spot market estimate of Helliwell's of some $55 million (Helliwell [1969, p. 101]). The gap between the spot and forward market estimates may reflect the degree to which estimates may be biased on account of simultaneity. Nevertheless, as with the U.K. results the forward market estimates for α tend to be greater than their spot market estimates in accordance with the analysis of simultaneous equations bias. In addition, the estimates of α for Canada do not support the 'perfect arbitrage school' although they are consistent with a relatively high degree of monetary integration.

When the exchange rate is flexible the final effect of an improvement in the uncovered differential (i.e. allowing for inelasticities in the supply of forward cover) by one percentage point is about $1600 m. When the exchange rate is fixed the final effect is only about $120 m, which compares closely with the final effect of $102 m for the U.K., which was measured over a period of fixed exchange rates. When the exchange rate is flexible about 80 per cent of official forward intervention would be reflected in spot inflows. However, when the exchange rate is fixed this proportion is more like 98 per cent because of the lower elasticity of forward market speculation when the exchange rate is fixed.

One would not expect there to be any differences between arbitrage responses under fixed and floating exchange rate regimes since exchange risk is in any event absent. Indeed, the difference between the respective estimates of α are not significantly different. The same cannot be said for the estimates of β where the speculation elasticity from the fixed rate regime is considerably smaller than its floating rate counterpart. However, here there is reason to believe that speculative responses might differ as between the two regimes since exchange risk could differ.

Two main conflicting arguments suggest themselves. First there is the argument that when the exchange rate is fixed there is a one-way option for the exchange rate. If it is undervalued the exchange rate can only appreciate, and vice versa. The one-way option therefore reduces the area of uncertainty, in which case the elasticity of the speculation schedule would be increased when the exchange rate is fixed.

The other main argument leads to the conclusion that the elasticity of the speculation schedule is likely to be higher when the exchange rate is floating since speculators do not have to contend with the added uncertainty of the authorities' behaviour. Therefore uncertainty is likely to be lower when the exchange rate is flexible and with it the value of β. (See the discussion on pp. 55–7.) Alternatively, when the exchange rate is freely floating the spot rate is likely to alter continuously so that if the authorities cannot maintain a disequilibrium exchange rate beyond the short run the speculator only has to forecast a sequence of relatively small exchange-rate changes in the floating case, whereas in the fixed case he has to forecast one sudden and large exchange-rate change. Indeed he might find the former a less daunting prospect than guessing not only how big the 'big bang' is likely to be when it comes, but also when it is likely to come.

The present results suggest that the factors that would tend to reduce β when the exchange rate is fixed dominate the factors that would tend to increase it implying that short-term capital flows are more responsive to monetary policy when exchange rates are floating than when they are fixed. If one assumes that α is invariant between fixed and floating exchange rate regimes, the results of Stoll [1968] also support this viewpoint since he finds that when the exchange rate is fixed the estimate of $\alpha/(\alpha + \beta)$ is greater than when the exchange rate is floating.

The estimates of $\alpha/(\alpha + \beta)$ in equations 6.6 and 6.7 may be compared with the results of previous researchers. The Canadian forward exchange market has been studied on several occasions but with the exception of Helliwell *et al*, [1971] nobody has used the EFA's forward position although the data have been available.

Author	Observation Period	$\alpha/(\alpha+\beta)$
Stoll [1968]	4.6.59–4.12.64	0.9869
„	4.6.59–26.4.62	0.9650
„	31.5.62–4.12.64	1.0154
Kesselman [1971]	1/53–11/60	0.490
„	4.7.55–28.11.60	0.34–0.79
Stein [1965]	2.1.59–26.4.62	0.561
Argy and Hodjera [1973]	1/58–12/64 ⎫	
„	1/66–6/67 ⎬	0.858
„	1/58–5/61	0.957
Helliwell et al. [1971]	1963 Q1–1968 Q4	0.59
McCallum [1977]	1/53–4/62	0.7415–0.9480

Because of the apparent sensitivity of the estimates of the specification of the expected spot rate, it is difficult to conclude whether these estimates conflict with the ones reported in this study. Of more interest is how $\alpha/(\alpha+\beta)$ varies as between fixed and floating rate estimation periods, to which reference has already been made. Since, as has been argued, it seems reasonable to restrict $\alpha/(\alpha+\beta)$ to be greater than 0.5, some of Kesselman's results seem doubtful, i.e. as with Hutton's results for sterling. Also Stoll's final result is too high since $\alpha/(\alpha+\beta)$ cannot be greater than unity. McCallum's results seem to be closest to our own.

The Forward French Franc 1963–1973

Unfortunately data on the French and German official forward positions were unavailable. Subsequently, the cases of the forward French Franc (FF) and the forward Deutsche Mark (DM) are less interesting than their British and Canadian counterparts. However, it is none the less of interest to explore the relative importance of arbitrage and speculation in the determination of these forward rates, especially since this constitutes almost virgin territory. In any event, as will be discussed in the next chapter, estimates of α can be obtained from the spot market, in which case β can be determined by substituting this estimate into the forward market estimate of $\alpha/(\alpha+\beta)$.

During the two-tier exchange market regime in France, from August 1971 through March 1974, it was appropriate to specify the 'financial' franc (compiled by the Bank of England) rather than the 'commercial' franc, since we are concerned with the capital account. However, since the two rates would tend to be related and since the market expected the two-tier system to be temporary, the suggested treatment of expectations would not require significant modification since the expected spot rate in the commercial market would reflect the relevant expected spot rate in the financial market.

The data are quarterly and are once again calculated as averages of end-month observations. The expected spot rate is specified along the lines discussed in equation 4.23 since during the observation period of 1963 Q1–1973 Q4 the franc was pegged. Indeed the precise form of this specification is as in equation 6.5. Because of the presence of a high degree of first-order serial correlation of the errors, the reported equation is expressed in first-differences:

$$\Delta F_t = 0.73861 + 0.88195\,\Delta\,(r_w - r_d + \hat{S})_t - 2.455\,\Delta D$$
$$\qquad\qquad (23.5) \qquad\qquad\qquad\qquad\qquad (5.31)$$
$$- \sum_{i=1}^{7} a_i\,\Delta\,RXP_{t-1} + \sum_{i=1}^{17} b_i\,\Delta\,VB_{t-i} \qquad (6.8)$$

a_i:

0.56247	7.1639	16.704	26.084	32.203	31.962	22.26
(0.063)	(0.059)	(1.34)	(2.05)	(2.33)	(2.32)	(2.21)

$$\sum = 136.94$$

b_i:

−0.0012748	−0.0014625	−0.0007389	0.00072036	0.0027396
(0.64)	(0.43)	(0.31)	(0.14)	(0.52)

0.005143	0.007755	0.0104	0.012902	0.015085	0.016774
(0.95)	(1.42)	(1.86)	(2.22)	(2.52)	(2.76)

0.017967	0.017119	0.015074	0.011656	0.0066903
(2.98)	(3.0)	(3.0)	(3.0)	(3.04)

$$\sum = 0.15434$$

$R^2 = 0.942 \qquad \sigma = 2.03 \qquad DW = 2.02$

where F and S are defined as in equation 6.5 in terms of the U.S. dollar (source: *IMF International Financial Statistics*). The domestic interest rate is represented by the three-month interbank rate (source: unpublished, Bank of England); RXP is conceived as in equation 6.5 (source of primary data: *OECD Historical Statistics*); and VB is the visible balance expressed in millions of U.S. dollars (source: *OECD Historical Statistics*). D is a dummy variable set equal to unity during political crises, e.g., May 1968. The equation suggests that these crises caused the covered differential to fall by about $2\frac{1}{2}$ percentage points. Both distributed lags were based on third-order polynomials with initial and final weights constrained to pass through zero.

Equation 6.8 indicates that all the principal explanatory variables are significant and have the correct sign. The estimate of $\alpha/(\alpha + \beta)$ suggests that the slope of the arbitrage schedule is seven-and-a-half times larger than the slope of the speculation schedule, which given the relative risks of speculation is plausible enough. The equation also lends support to the rational expectations hypothesis.

Argy and Hodjera [1973] estimate $\alpha/(\alpha+\beta)$ at 0.7. However, their estimates are likely to be biased downwards because they assume a one-to-one relationship between changes in the spot rate and changes in the forward rate.

The Forward Deutsche Mark 1960–1972

The previous exercise is repeated in the case of the forward DM using quarterly data from 1960 Q1–1972 Q4. A difficulty relates to the temporary float of the DM in May 1970. However, its brevity and the understanding that the 'float' was a device for determining a new peg would mean that no special difficulties are raised. A representative equation is reported:

$$F_t = 32.4 + 0.968(r_w - r_d + \hat{S})_t + \sum_{i=1}^{10} a_i \Delta RES_{t-1}$$
$$(17.7)$$

$$+ \sum_{i=1}^{10} b_i RXP_{t-i} \tag{6.9}$$

a_i	0.000489	0.000341	0.000284	0.000293	0.000342
	(1.9)	(1.94)	(1.69)	(1.8)	(2.15)
	0.000404	0.000454	0.000464	0.000409	0.000263
	(2.31)	(2.15)	(1.94)	(1.79)	(1.67)

$\Sigma = 0.00375$

b_i	−12.44	−9.22	−6.45	−4.11	−2.21	−.747	.279	.865
	(2.04)	(2.3)	(2.6)	(2.27)	(1.1)	(0.31)	(0.11)	(0.34)

$.1.01$ $.726$ $\Sigma = -32.3$
(0.5) (0.17)

$R^2 = 0.93$

$\sigma = 2.06$

$DW = 1.66$

where all data are conceived as in equation 6.5. Exchange rate and interest rate data were taken from the *Deutsche Bundesbank Monthly*

Review. The domestic interest rate was represented by the three month money market rate in Frankfurt. *RXP* once again is as in equation 6.5. (primary source: *OECD Historical Statistics*). ΔRES is the change in the reserves expressed in millions of U.S. dollars (source: *OECD Historical Statistics*) which replaces the visible balance as the 'pressure' variable in the expected spot rate specification. The first distributed lag was estimated, using a third order polynomial with the final weight constrained to pass through zero. The second distributed lag was estimated, using a second order polynomial on the same basis. In this and all the other equations, the appropriate polynomial and restrictions were determined largely on the basis of their effect on the standard error of estimate.

Equation 6.9 suggesting that if the Bundesbank were to buy DM100 forward, there would be a spot inflow, ceteris paribus, of DM 96.8. In other words, because the forward rate is so heavily influenced by covered-interest arbitrage these transactions largely take place with covered-interest arbitrageurs. The equation also confirms the influences of the specification of rational expectations as in equation 4.23.

Argy and Hodjera [1973] estimated that in the case of the DM $\alpha/(\alpha + \beta)$ was 0.79. When it is considered that this estimate is likely to be biased downwards, since it assumes a one-to-one relationship between the spot and the forward rate, it is most probably not too different from the estimate in equation 6.9.

Assessment

The results represented in equations 6.5–6.9 suggest a number of conclusions that are of direct relevance to policy.

(i) The Canadian and British results imply that the capital account is not very sensitive to interest-rate changes. In fact it is perhaps surprisingly insensitive because covered-interest arbitrage is not as elastic as it might be and the speculative supply of forward exchange is inelastic. An increase in domestic interest rates in the U.K. by one percentage point is likely to add $102 millions to the capital account and in Canada the figure is about $120 millions.

(ii) However, the capital account is likely to be highly sensitive to forward intervention, *ceteris paribus*, for precisely the same reasons that the capital account is likely to be interest-insensitive. Indeed, this conclusion is reinforced by the results for France and West Germany where the ratio of $\alpha/(\alpha + \beta)$ was fairly high.

(iii) The Canadian results suggest that the elasticity of supply of forward exchange is likely to fall when the exchange rate is fixed and the authorities are intervening in the spot market. Recalling the discussion on pp. 55–7, this suggests that exchange rate intervention will have a destabilising influence on the spot market and that in these respects intervention would be self-defeating.

(iv) With the exception of the Canadian results, the version of the rational expectations hypothesis under fixed exchange rates enjoyed a respectable degree of empirical support.

7 Econometric Analyses of Capital Movements

In the previous chapter an attempt was made to form a consensus on the nature of forward exchange activity based on some international evidence. In many respects the present chapter is a sequel, in so far as we review some new international evidence regarding transactions in the spot market.

We begin by considering the determination of short-term capital movements in the balance of payments of the United Kingdom, France and West Germany. In particular, the objective here is to estimate relationships based on equation 2.18 out of which a number of interesting issues may be identified.

(i) It has already been pointed out on pp. 79–81 that the covered interest arbitrage schedule may be estimated either through an analysis of the forward market or through an analysis of the spot market. It was concluded that the forward market estimate might be biased upwards and the spot market market estimate biased downwards if simultaneity is not adequately treated. In other words, the two estimates, if they differ, may serve the purpose of providing a range inside which the true value of the covered-interest arbitrage schedule might lie. The forward estimate would serve as an upper bound, and the spot market estimate would serve as a lower bound. Consequently, estimates of equation 2.18 would yield lower bound estimates for α. Hopefully, of course, the two estimates will not be significantly different from each other. Since the Canadian data on spot market transactions are not included in this chapter, this exercise may only be performed with respect to the results for the United Kingdom.

(ii) Because forward intervention data were not available, estimates of the speculation schedule in the forward exchange market could not be obtained in the French and West German cases in the previous chapter. However, armed with an estimate for α from the spot market, we may indirectly solve for β via the estimate for $\alpha/(\alpha + \beta)$ from the respective forward market equations 6.8 and 6.9. This will provide an indication of the combined effects of risk and risk aversion in the forward market.

(iii) The capital account may also be sensitive to changes in uncovered differentials in their own right and not merely via their effects on covered arbitrage through their impact on covered interest differentials. That is to say, investors may speculate directly in the spot market by investing on the basis of uncovered interest rate differentials and their expectations regarding future exchange rate developments. In equation 2.17 the slope of the uncovered arbitrage or spot speculation schedule is denoted by γ which may be estimated via equation 2.18. This parameter has a direct relevance for policy since most monetary authorities will be interested in the likely effect on the balance of payments of their interest rate policies.

(iv) Since it is necessary to specify the expected spot rate to estimate equation 2.18 an opportunity is presented further to investigate alternative approaches to the formation of exchange rate expectations. In particular, attention is focused once more on the rational expectations hypothesis.

It is curious to note that much of the theoretical and empirical literature on the capital account of the balance of payments has seemed to concern itself with short-term capital movements and that other aspects of the capital account have been somewhat neglected, although there are exceptions e.g. Branson [1968]. There is, of course, a definitional problem regarding where short-term capital flows end and long-term capital flows begin. If short-term capital flows are defined as those flows that are sensitive to interest rates, exchange rate expectations etc. while long-term flows are defined as those which are not, then the conceptual issue will be clear. On the other hand, in this case very few flows are likely to be long-term and most probably 'the short-term capital movements' with which previous econometric investigators have been concerned, e.g. Hodjera [1971], Hutton [1977], are unduly narrow.

In the present study long-term capital movements are defined as those flows that are sensitive to long-term interest rates, while short-term capital movements are responsive to short-term interest rates. There is of course a third category which is responsive to neither set of interest rates. This approach opens up an additional set of policy considerations for the authorities since they could assign short-term interest rates to the short end of the capital account and long-term interest rates to the long end. In the past, however, it would seem that the monetary authorities have tended to consider the former assignment almost to the total exclusion of the latter assignment. This may have been a matter of conscious choice. On the other hand, it may also have been based on a lack of knowledge about the determinants of long-term capital movements.

To this end, various attempts are made to estimate relationships based on equation 2.21. In particular, attention is focused on the relationship between long-term interest rates at home and overseas and long-term capital flows on the balance of payments. An obvious institutional difference between short and long-term capital flows is that beyond a six to twelve-month horizon (for further details see the next chapter) there are no forward exchange markets to speak of, in which case long-term capital flows take place directly on the spot market. This means that investors at the long end have to incur their own exchange risk directly; they cannot contract out their exchange risk to forward market speculators as is the case with short-term capital flows. Since exchange risk is likely to dampen the response of capital movements to interest rate changes, it should be considered whether the absence of longer-term forward exchange markets is likely to dampen the response of long-term capital movements to interest rate changes.

Most probably, the forward exchange markets imply a degree of specialisation in exchange risk taking since it is likely that some operators will speculate on an outright basis. Therefore, from this point of view the absence of long-term forward exchange speculation may reduce the interest sensitivity of the capital account at the long end. In addition the variance of the expected spot rate is likely to increase with the period to which the expectations refer as indicated by equation 4.21 when expectations are formed rationally. If so, this would further inhibit the interest sensitivity of the capital account at the long end. On the other hand, in some respects it may be easier to predict the more distant future than the immediate future, in which case the sensitivity would be enhanced. This possibility arises when it is considered that it may be easier to forecast the long term—where, as it were, the chickens come home to roost—than the short term, where there could be considerable uncertainty about the nature of lagged responses which would be relevant to short-term forecasting.

Short-term Capital Flows

(i) *The United Kingdom* 1964-73

The following equation was estimated using quarterly data from 1964 Q2 – 1974 Q4.

$$STC_t = 54 + 300\Delta C\hat{D}_t + 48\Delta UD_t + 6\Delta \hat{S}^e_t \qquad (7.1)$$
$$\quad (5.8) \qquad (5.8) \qquad (5.8)$$

$$-211\,Q1 - 192\,Q3 - 935\,CRIS$$
$$\quad (2.5) \qquad (2.2) \qquad (3.8)$$

$$+\frac{\varepsilon_t}{1 + .078B - .381\,B^2}$$
$$\qquad (.4) \qquad (2.3)$$

$$R^2 = 0.76, \quad \sigma = \pounds 190\text{m}, \qquad DW = 1.81,$$
$$OP;\ 1964\ Q2 - 1973\ Q4$$

where all coefficients are in £ millions ad where Q1 and Q3 are quarterly dummies for the first and third quarters respectively and *CRIS* is a speculative dummy specified as:

CRIS: Speculation dummy:

1966	Q3	0.5	Run on £
1969	Q3	0.5	£ affected by devaluations of franc
1971	Q4	−0.5	Run on $ (pre-Smithsonian)
1972	Q2	1.0	Run before £ floated
1973	Q1	−0.5	Run on $

This dummy was specified on a crude if pragmatic basis. The dummy was entered with appropriate sign for periods where speculation was exceptionally rife such as prior to the devaluation in 1967 and before sterling was floated in 1972. In the absence of the dummy, the model can at best only pick up trends in speculative patterns. The dummy was scaled to reflect the intensity of the crisis. The coefficient on the dummy implies that a full-scale crisis will cause a short-term capital outflow of approaching £1 billion.

Short Term Capital Flows (STC) (source: *Economic Trends*, Central Statistical Office, London) are defined as follows in £millions: 'Other borrowing or lending net by UK banks in foreign currency' + 'exchange reserves in Sterling: Banking and money market liabilities (excluding holdings of international organizations)' + other external banking and money market liabilities in Sterling' + 'external Sterling claims' + 'other commercial short-term transactions net' + 'balancing item'. The balancing item is included on the assumption that it may be influenced by leads and lags which in turn would be explained by factors influencing short-term capital flows.

$\widehat{CD}$, the covered differential, is defined as $r_d - \hat{S} - r_w + \hat{F}$ using the definitions of equation 6.5, where F is the estimate of F from that equation.

$\Delta \hat{S}^e$ is the estimate of the change in the expected spot rate from equation 6.5 i.e.

$$\Delta \hat{S}^e = \Delta\left[F - \frac{\hat{\alpha}}{\alpha + \beta} \ (\hat{S} - UD) - \frac{\hat{1}}{\alpha + \beta}G \right] \ \frac{(\alpha + \beta)}{\beta} \ (7.2)$$

This procedure avoids the necessity of rationalising different models of expectations in the various equations of the model. On the other hand it is flexible since $\Delta \hat{S}^e$ is specified with respect to an unrestricted distributed lag.

B denotes the backward operator. The errors indicated a second-order autoregressive process. While many variables proved to be significant in their own right, collinearity within certain groups of variables upset coefficients when variables were entered on an unweighted basis. Variables were therefore weighted together and alternative weighting schemes were selected on the basis of F tests. The final weighting pattern is reported.

Equation 7.1 suggests that $\hat{\alpha}$ equals 300 and that $\hat{\gamma}$ equals 48. In other words if the covered differential improves by one percentage point the capital account will experience a once-and-for-all inflow of £300 million. If the uncovered differential improves by one percentage point it will improve by £48 million. Since uncovered arbitrage will inevitably be riskier than covered arbitrage these results (unlike Hutton [1977]) bear out the *a priori* expectation that α should be greater than γ, just in the same way as α should be greater than β (again unlike Hutton [1977]) in the estimation of equation 2.15.

The estimate of α from equation 6.5 when converted at an exchange rate typical for the estimation period (£1 = \$2.4) is about 800. This compares with an estimate of 300 from the spot market. However, it should be recalled that since the forward market estimate for α is the ratio of two parameter estimates, its confidence interval is fairly wide and the two estimates for α are less different than they appear. Nevertheless, they may serve as the upper and lower bounds for α along the lines discussed on p. 93.

Therefore, these results do not support the Cambist or 'perfect arbitrage school' since even the upper bound estimate for α is not particularly large.

Other estimates for α are reported in terms of the effects of a one percentage point change in the covered differential on desired short-term capital flows:

	£million
Hodjera [1971, p. 757]	921
Branson and Hill [1971, p. 29]	140
Minford [1975, p. 121]	91
Hutton [1977, pp. 36–7]	96

Hodjera's estimate is by far the highest. The other three estimates lie remarkably close together and are surprisingly low. However, despite their differences the results have one important aspect in common; they all contradict the Cambist view that α should be a fairly large number.

Finally, since $\Delta\hat{S}^e$ is derived from a previous specification of the rational expectations hypothesis, equation 7.1 lends further support to the view that in the case of the U.K. at least exchange rate expectations are formed rationally.

(ii) France 1967–73
Unfortunately, quarterly time series on the behaviour of the French capital account date back only as far as the first quarter of 1967. Subsequently the French capital flows equations are rather short on degrees of freedom (about 20). Nevertheless, the investigation seemed

worthwhile, especially since these data had apparently not been studied before, and the results are fairly encouraging. French capital account data were obtained from 'Balance des Paiements de l'Année – entre la France et l'Extérieur' (Ministère de l'Economie; Banque de France) are measured in millions of French francs (FF). Short-term capital flows (STC) are defined to cover flows of the 'secteur privé non-bancaire' and the 'secteur bancaire' for 'capitaux à court terme et liquides'. Flows of the 'secteur public' are omitted since they are unlikely to be sensitive to interest rates etc. STC also includes 'erreurs et omissions' since these are likely to reflect leads and lags which as speculative flows belong naturally in STC, i.e., for reasons analogous to the inclusion of the 'balancing item' in the case of U.K. short-term capital flows. The French data are measured 'en termes de règlements' rather than 'en termes de transactions' in which case they do not include trade credit. In these respects they are comparable to the U.K. data where trade credit had been omitted. (Separate equations for the determination of U.K. trade credit may be found in Beenstock [1976, pp. 126–30].)

A representative equation is reported:

$$STC_t = 172 + 267.21 \Delta \widehat{CD}_t + 3640.6 \Delta D - \sum_{i=1}^{14} a_i \Delta RXP_{t-i}$$
$$\quad\quad (7.05) \quad\quad\quad (15.4) \quad\quad\quad$$
$$+ \sum_{i=1}^{12} b_i \Delta VB_{t-i} \quad\quad\quad\quad\quad\quad\quad\quad (7.3)$$

a_i :

37279	39710	43785	48749	53851	58337
(7.67)	(10.28)	(13.5)	(16.8)	17.92)	15.96)

61453	62447	60556	55057	45166	30140	9227
(13.18)	(10.83)	(8.98)	(7.38)	(5.82)	(3.95)	(1.28)

$$\Sigma = 605217$$

b_i :

2.9906	5.4827	7.4764	8.9717	9.9685	10.467
(3.93)	(3.93)	(3.93)	(3.93)	(3.93)	(3.93

10.467	9.9685	8.9717	7.4764	5.4827	2.9906
(3.93)	(3.93)	(3.93)	(3.93)	(3.93)	(3.93

$$\Sigma = 90.71$$

$R^2 = 0.958 \quad \sigma = \text{FF822m} \quad DW = 2.11$

$OP = 196701{-}1973Q4$

$\rho_1 = -0.911 \quad\quad \rho_2 = -0.928$
$\quad (8.84) \quad\quad\quad\quad (9.98)$

where the covered differential $(\hat{CD})$ is defined as in equation 7.1 from data already discussed in connection with equation 6.8. The speculative dummy (D) and the specification of the expected exchange rate are also as in equation 6.8. The speculative dummy suggests that political crises were associated with short-term capital outflows of about FF 3.64 billions. However, the specification implies that this money is likely to return once the crisis is past. The distributed lag on relative export prices (RXP) was estimated on the basis of a third order polynomial. The distributed lag structure on the 'pressure' variable, the change in the visible balance $(\Delta V\dot{B})$ was estimated on the basis of a quadratic polynomial with first and last weights constrained to pass through zero. A second order autoregressive error model was estimated. Since the roots of this model are less than one, the disturbance structure is stationary. Finally, the dependent variable is denominated in millions of French francs (FF).

The specification in equation 7.3 does not distinguish between the covered and uncovered differentials as was the case with equation 7.1. Subsequently, separate estimates of α and γ cannot be derived. The difficulty here is that the uncovered differential and the cost of forward cover are highly correlated. Subsequently, the value for α is likely to be less than 267.21 since no doubt some of this may be attributed to the response of uncovered arbitrage (γ). In other words, if the covered differential improves by one percentage point, the French balance of payments is likely to experience a short-term capital inflow of something less than FF 267.21 millions which is most probably too low a sum to support the Cambist or 'perfect arbitrage' school. It is worth noting, however, that when the speculative dummy was excluded, the coefficient on the change in the covered differential rose to 710, but its t value fell to 2.5 and the standard error of estimate significantly deteriorated.

Other estimates of the effects of an improvement in the covered differential by one percentage point have been:

Branson and Hill [1971, pp. 32–3]	FF 1000 millions
Antier [1973, p. 53]	FF 950 millions

i.e. roughly equal to the present results when, as with these studies, the speculative dummy is ignored. On the other hand, given the disparity in the data definitions it is difficult to make very meaningful comparisons. However, all these results seem to conflict with the Cambist doctrine, which has traditionally been a French school of thought.

If we assume that α is about 267, then from equation 6.8 where the estimate for $\alpha/(\alpha + \beta)$ is 0.882, β would be equal to 35.7. In other words, if the expected spot rate is expected to increase at an annual rate of 1 per cent per year, the speculative demand for forward French francs will increase by about FF 35.7 millions, which is a relatively low figure. This means that the forward market speculation schedule is inelastic and that changes in the uncovered differential are likely to have only a minor impact on the French capital account. For example, equation 6.8 suggests that if French short-term interest rates rise by one (annual) percentage point, the covered differential will only rise by 0.118 per cent, which through equation 7.3 would generate a short-term capital inflow of only about FF 31.5 millions. Under any interpretation this is a very low figure.

As equation 6.8, equation 7.3 lends further support for the version of the rational expectations hypothesis in equation 4.23. Both the underlying expectations variable (ΔRXP) and the 'pressure' variable (ΔVB) are quite significant.

(iii) *West Germany 1961–72*

Like the French data on capital movements, the German data have apparently not been seriously explored. However, in the German case there is an abundance of data. The quarterly results in equation (7.4) refer to 'private short-term capital transactions net', as in the *Deutsche Bundesbank Monthly Review*, and are measured in DM millions. However, as with the French and British data, the West German data incorporate 'unidentified transactions' since they are comparable to 'erreurs et omissions' and the 'balancing item'. A single representative result is reported:

$$STC_t = 1075 + 685.5\Delta\hat{CD}_t + \sum_{i=1}^{18} a_i \Delta VB_{t-1} \qquad (7.4)$$
$$(5.62)$$

a_i :

−1.012	−0.7411	−0.495	−0.2747	−0.07947
(3.6)	(3.06)	(2.32)	(1.39)	(0.42)
0.0905	0.235	0.355	0.4488	0.5177
(0.48)	(1.21)	(1.78)	(2.21)	(2.54)
0.5613	0.5796	0.5727	0.5404	0.4829
(2.79)	(2.99)	(3.14)	(3.26)	(3.36)
0.4	0.292	0.1586	$\Sigma = 2.632$	
(3.45)	(3.52)	(3.58)		

$R^2 = 0.599$, $\sigma = $ DM2453m, $OP = $ 1962 Q2–1972 Q4, $DW = 1.9$

where the covered differential ($\hat{CD}$) is defined as in equation 7.1 and constructed from data already discussed in equation 6.9. The lag structure was estimated on the basis of a quadratic polynomial with the final weight constrained to pass through zero.

As with equation 7.3, the covered and uncovered differentials are not distinguished and the coefficient on $\Delta\widehat{CD}$ will not be a pure estimate of α since uncovered arbitrage will be reflected in this coefficient too, given the close correlation between changes in the covered and uncovered differentials. However, we can conclude that α will be less than 685.5 and that an improvement in the covered differential by one percentage point is likely to generate a covered capital inflow of no more than DM 685.5 millions. As with the British, French and Canadian results, this sum is not large enough to be consistent with the 'perfect arbitrage school'. Indeed, it is fairly small and in line with other estimates. Branson and Hill [1971, pp. 34–5] estimate this response at DM 880 millions and Porter [1972, p. 406] estimates it at DM 770 millions. However, using monthly data Porter finds a two-quarter effect of DM 2320 millions.

If we assume that $\alpha = 685.5$, then from the estimate of $\alpha/(\alpha + \beta)$ in equation 6.9 we find that β, the slope of speculation schedule in the forward market is 22.7. This means that if the expected change in the DM increases by one annual percentage point, the speculative demand for forward DM will rise by DM 22.7 millions, which is once again a low figure. This means that changes in uncovered differentials are unlikely to exert a large influence on the West German balance of payments. For example, combining the results of equations 6.9 and 7.4, if short-term interest rates rise by one annual percentage point, the covered differential would only improve by 0.032 per cent, generating a short-term inflow of about DM 22 millions. By any criterion this must be considered as a small response.

The specification in equation 7.4 indicates that it was not possible to achieve satisfactory results on the basis of the rational expectations hypothesis. At least, it was not possible to continue an underlying expectations variable with a 'pressure' variable. However, the change in the visible balance performed fairly well on its own and this specification compares with Hutton's [1977, p. 33]. The initial negative weights could be attributed to the argument that improvements in the visible balance on account of relative price effects would lead to expected depreciations. In other words, the estimated lag structure may be influenced by the covariance between RXP and VB. In the long run the equation suggests that if the visible balance improves by $100 millions per quarter (or approximately DM 400 millions), there will be a short-term capital inflow of about DM 263 millions. This supports the conventional view that the West German capital account has been heavily influenced by speculative capital movements during the 1960s and early 1970s.

Long-term Capital Flows

(i) *The United Kingdom 1964–74:*
In this section we report various attempts to estimate equation 2.21.

Equation 7.5 refers to 'long-term inward capital movements', defined as 'inward private investment: direct' + 'U.K. company securities' (issued for domestic use) + 'miscellaneous capital' (domestic use only), i.e. portfolio borrowing to finance outward investment is excluded (source: *Economic Trends*, C.S.O., London, and Bank of England). In this category inward direct investment and inward portfolio investment are combined. However, it should be emphasised that the inward direct investment is conceived in balance of payments terms and not in terms of capital formation. For example, capital formation in the U.K. by a foreign subsidiary would not appear as 'inward direct investment' unless the finance was arranged by the parent overseas. Consequently, 'inward direct investment' is likely to depend on relative interest rates rather than relative rates of return on capital and of course on the policies of international corporations in respect of the centralisation of their financial operations. (Apparently this was not recognised in Boatwright and Renton's [1975] study of direct investment in the U.K. balance of payments.) Portfolio investment is also likely to depend on the relative expected returns on portfolio investment in the U.K. For this reason inward direct and portfolio investment have been aggregated under 'inward long-term capital movements' (*LTC*). Inflows would tend to occur when the long-term interest rate differential changes and when the expected rate of exchange rate depreciation falls. We report the following equation:

$$LTC_t = \sum_{i=1}^{12} a_i \Delta UDL_{t-i+1} + \sum_{j=1}^{4} b_j \Delta \hat{S}^e_{t-j+1}$$
$$+ \sum_{k=1}^{4} c_K \Delta P_{w\,t-k+1} \tag{7.5}$$
$$+ 47.81 + \frac{e_t}{1 - .262B}$$
$$(1.6)$$

i	a_i		j	b_j	
1.	− 376	(3.04)	1.	1.92	(4.61)
2.	− 336	(3.30)	2.	1.44	(4.61)
3.	− 297	(3.38)	3.	.96	(4.61)
4.	− 260	(3.23)	4.	.48	(4.61)
5.	− 224	(2.88)	Total	4.80	
6.	− 190	(2.47)			
7.	− 158	(2.09)	k	c_k	
8.	− 128	(1.76)	1	8.64	(5.22)
9.	− 99	(1.50)	2.	6.48	(5.22)
10.	− 72	(1.28)	3.	4.32	(5.22)
11.	− 46	(1.11)	4.	2.16	(5.22)
12.	− 22	(.97)	Total	21.6	
Total	2208				

$\sigma = £\,53.3\text{m}$ $R^2 = .577$ $DW = 2.1$ $OP = 1964\,Q1\text{--}1974\,Q2$

where UDL is the long-term uncovered differential expressed as the ratio of the euro-bond rate (source: Bank of England) to the rate of interest on War Loan (source: *Bank of England Quarterly Bulletin*). These data were expressed as averages of end-month observations since the data are quarterly.

$\hat{S}^e$, the estimate of the expected spot rate, was derived through equation 7.2. ΔP_w is the change in world prices (primary source: *OECD Historical Statistics*) which proxies changes in overseas monetary wealth (attempts to include this effect in previous equations failed). The coefficients on relative interest rates were estimated by a second order polynomial constrained to pass through zero at $t-13$. The lag structures for $\Delta \hat{S}^e$ and ΔP_w were both estimated by first-order polynomials constrained to pass through zero at $t-5$. This polynomial involves the estimation of only one parameter and results in the same t value for each lag coefficient. The long lag on ΔUDL has a variety of interpretations. First, long-term capital movements as here defined reflect the financial policies of the international corporations and these policies are unlikely to respond fully to interest rate movements in the very short term. The decision to finance the operations of affiliates in the UK in foreign currency rather than in sterling is more likely to be related to a moving average of relative borrowing costs. Secondly, LTC includes equity capital and in the long run relative equity yields may be expected to be related to relative long-term bond yields. Hence, the three-year lag structure might reflect this long-term relationship. The equation indicates that in the long run a rise in U.K. long-term interest rates from 14 per cent to 15 per cent would induce an inflow of £100 million if euro-bond rates were 8 per cent. If U.K. interest rates were 10 per cent a 1 per cent rise would produce an inflow of £160 million. A 1 per cent rise in world prices (equivalent to an annual rate of 4 per cent) would produce an inflow of £13 million in the quarter in which it occurred and an inflow of £32 million after one year.

The specification for the change in the expected spot rate is also statistically significant and since it is based on equation 4.23 this is the third equation where U.K. data have lent support to the hypothesis that expectations are formed rationally.

An additional equation regarding the long-term capital account in the U.K. is reported where we consider the overseas demand for gilt-edged securities (BGS) which consists of the private demand and the official demand of central monetary institutions. Here too we would expect that BGS was related to changes in interest rate differentials and changes in the expected rate of depreciation. The most respectable equation was:

$$BGS_t = 3 - 260\,\Delta UDL_t + 0.043\,\Delta RESOSA_t \qquad (7.6)$$
$$(1.9) \qquad\quad (2.4)$$

$$+ 1.28 \Delta \hat{S}^e_{t-1} + \frac{\varepsilon_t}{1 - 0.334B - 0.307B^2}$$
$$\quad (2.6) \qquad\qquad (2.06) \quad (1.88)$$

$$R^2 = 0.33 \quad \sigma = £42m \quad DW = 2.12$$
$$OP = 1964\ Q1\text{--}1973\ Q4$$

BGS is defined as 'overseas investment in the U.K. public sector: British government securities and local authority mortgages and securities' + 'exchange reserves in sterling: British government securities' (excluding international organisations). (Source: *Economic Trends*, C.S.O., London.)

RESOSA denotes the reserves (measured in £ millions) of the Overseas Sterling Area countries who over the observation period were important holders of sterling. The equation suggests that about 4.3 per cent of their reserve increases were held in gilt-edged securities.

The coefficient on ΔUDL is barely significant. The equation implies that if U.K. long-term interest rates rise from 10 per cent to 11 per cent when overseas long-term interest rates are 8 per cent, the overseas demand for gilt-edged stock would rise by about £18.9 millions. The specification of the expected spot rate continues to perform reasonably well.

The residuals indicated a second order autoregressive process and the percentage of explained variance was low.

Thus, when U.K. long-term interest rates rise by one annual percentage point, the long-term capital account improves by about £180 millions after the full adjustment. Equations 6.5 and 7.1 imply that when short-term interest rates rise by one percentage point, the short-term capital account improves by about £64 millions. This evidence suggests that the long-term capital account is more interest-sensitive than the short-term capital account.

(ii) France 1967–73

As with the British results it was necessary to estimate a distributed lag on the change in the long-term uncovered differential:

$$LTC_t = -67.27 + 649.9\Delta D + \sum_{i=0}^{7} a_i \Delta LUD_{t-i}$$
$$\qquad\qquad (2.58)$$

$$- \sum_{i=1}^{8} b_i \Delta RXP_{t-i} \qquad\qquad (7.7)$$

a_i :

283	567.85	823.44	1018.6	1122.4	1103.5	930.86
(0.65)	(0.93)	(1.34)	(1.89)	(2.34)	(2.28)	(1.95)

573.4 $\Sigma = 6423$
(1.65)

b_1 : 18841   21939   18503   11741   4859.4   1064.3   3562.5
        (2.48)   (3.5)   (2.81)   (1.58)   (0.5)   (0.1)   (0.32)

        15561 $\Sigma = 96070$
        (1.57)

$R^2 = 0.834$ $\sigma = $ FF 659.9m   DW = 2.03 $\rho_1 = 0.522$
                                                                    (2.6)
$OP = 1967$ Q1–1973 Q4

where LTC is 'capitaux à long terme' excluding the 'secteur public' (source: Balance de Paiements de l'Année – entre la France et l'Extérieur Ministère de l'Economie; Banque de France) and is measured in millions of French francs. The data are quarterly.

D is the speculative dummy as in equations 6.8 and 7.3. LUD is the long-term uncovered differential expressed as the difference between domestic and overseas long-term interest rates (i.e. unlike UDL, which is a ratio). The domestic interest rate is proxied by the yield on long-term government bonds (source: IMF, *Internationl Financial Statistics*) and the overseas interest rate by the yield on long-term U.S. Government bonds (source: IMF, *International Financial Statistics*). The interest rate data are expressed as averages of end-month observations. RXP is once more the ratio of French export prices to those of her principal competitors.

The distributed lag on ΔLUD was estimated on the basis of a third-order polynomial with initial and end-weights constrained to pass through zero. The distributed lag on ΔRXP was also estimated on the basis of a cubic polynomial but with the initial and end-weights being freely determined.

The surprising feature about this equation is the very high long-term response of capital movements to changes in the long-term uncovered differential. The equation suggests that if this differential improves in favour of France by one percentage point, there would be an inflow on the French capital account of about FF 6.4 billions spread over two years. The length of this lag is roughly the same as in equation 7.5 for the U.K. and may be explained along similar lines. However, the size of the coefficient is considerably greater. This inflow compares with a short-term capital inflow under the same circumstances of only FF 31.5 millions as discussed on p. 99. Even though the coefficients on ΔLUD are barely significant, it is curious to note that, as with the U.K. results, the French results are suggestive of a greater sensitivity of the long-term capital account to interest rate changes.

In equation 7.7 it was not possible successfully to specify equation 4.23 as the expected spot rate. However, the specification of ΔRXP was moderately successful even if the lag structure is somewhat erratic towards the end. The equation implies that if French export price rise by

1 per cent relative to overseas prices, there will be a long-term capital outflow of about FF 96 millions. Finally, during speculative crisis the long-term capital account deteriorated by about FF 650 millions.

(iii) West Germany 1960–72:

A representative equation is reported that was estimated over the period 1960 Q2–1972 Q4:

$$LTC_t = -313 + \sum_{i=0}^{9} a_i \Delta LUD_{t-i} + \sum_{i=0}^{9} b_i \Delta S_{t-i} \qquad (7.8)$$

a_i :

432.4	778.3	1037.2	1211	1297.1	1297.1
(3.85)	(3.85)	(3.85)	(3.85)	(3.85)	(3.85)

1211	1037.7	778.3	432.4	$\Sigma = 9511$
(3.85)	(3.85)	(3.85)	(3.85)	

b_1 :

65.3	61.9	89.4	136	189.9	239.1	271.8
(2.27)	(1.36)	(1.51)	(2.0)	(2.52)	(2.9)	(3.11)

276.1	240.1	152	$\Sigma = 1721.6$
(3.19)	(3.2)	(3.18)	

$R^2 = 0.724$ $\sigma = \text{DM} 1302\text{m}$ $OP = 1960$ Q2–1972 Q4

$DW = 1.91$ $\rho = 0.514$
    (4.08)

where *LTC* is 'private long-term capital transactions net' in DM millions (source: *Deutsche Bundesbank Monthly Review*). The long-term uncovered differential (*LUD*) is once more expressed against the yield on long-term U.S. bonds and the domestic rate is represented by the yield on long-term government bonds (source: IMF, *International Financial Statistics*). Since the data are quarterly, *LUD* is expressed as an average of end-month observations. *S* is the spot rate as defined following equation 6.5.

The lag structure on ΔLUD is based on a quadratic polynomial with first and final weights constrained to pass through zero. The lag structure on ΔS is based on a cubic polynomial with the final weight constrained to pass through zero.

Equation 7.8 is strikingly similar to equation 7.7 for France in that it suggests that, like the French capital account, the German capital account is relatively interest-sensitive at the long end, and experimentation indicated that a ten-quarter lag was optimal in terms of goodness of fit. The equation suggests that if the long-term uncovered

differential moves in favour of West Germany by one annual percentage
point, the German capital account will impprove by about DM 9.5
billions in a $2\frac{1}{2}$ year period. This compares with an effect of only DM22
millions at the short end, as discussed on p. 101. Whether or not the
precise orders of magnitude are correct here may be less important than
the qualitative inference regarding the relative interest-sensitivity of the
long-term capital account.

Indeed, this influence is consistent with previous researches. Branson
and Hill [1971, p. 35] similarly find the German capital account to be
more responsive to long-term interest rates than to short-term interest
rates. They found the effect of an improvement of the long-term
uncovered differential by one percentage point to be DM3000m.
Unfortunately, there have not even been crude attempts to examine the
effect of long-term interest rates on the French capital account. So we
have no basis for comparison regarding the French estimates.

The other feature of equation 7.8 is the complete failure to fit a
specification of equation 4.23. Instead, lagged values of the spot rate were
specified on the assumption that the expected spot rate is a weighted
average of past values of the spot rate. However, as Muth [1960] has
discussed, under certain circumstances the regressive-extrapolative
model will coincide with the set of weights which rationally connect the
past with the future. It is not possible to check this possibility regarding
equation 7.8.

Summary

In this section we summarise some of the main results from this and the
preceding chapter. Table 7.1 summarises the principal parameter
estimates converted into a common currency (millions of U.S.$) for
purposes of comparison.

TABLE 7.1   Parameter Estimates ($ millions)

	α	β	γ	δ[e]
U.K.[a]	720(1929)[f]	103	115.2	432[g]
France[b]	48.5	6.5		1164
W. Germany[c]	171.4	5.67		2375
Canada[d]	5803[f]	107		

[a] £1 = $2.4;   [b] FF 5.5 = $1;   [c] DM4 = $1;   [d] CAN$1 = $1   [e] long-run
effect;   [f] forward market estimate;   [g] approximate value because of non-linear
specification.

The parameters in Table 7.1 are:

- α : the slope of the covered interest arbitrage schedule as in equation 2.12.
- β : the slope of the forward market speculation schedule as in equation 2.13.
- γ : the slope of the uncovered interest arbitrage or spot speculation schedule as in equation 2.17.
- δ : the slope of the long-term uncovered interest arbitrage schedule as in equation 2.21.

All these parameters refer to the effects of a change of one annual percentage point in the appropriate variable. For example, the α value for France implies that when the French covered interest rate differential rises by one percentage point, covered arbitrage positions are likely to increase by about $48.5 millions. The exchange rate assumptions are representative of exchange rates against the U.S. dollar during the estimation period. The estimates for α and β for Canada are taken from the fixed exchange rate period for comparison with the other estimates. However, attention has already been drawn to the fact that during the period of floating exchange rates the Canadian estimate for β was considerably larger (see p. 87).

The striking feature about the values for α in Table 7.1 is the low estimates for France and Germany as compared with the estimates for Canada and the U.K. despite the fact that during the observation period the GDPs of France and Germany (measured in U.S. dollars) were higher than in the U.K. and Canada. The Canadian figures is of course a forward market estimate and is not strictly comparable with the spot market estimates. However, Helliwell *et al.* [1969, p. 101] have a spot market estimate of $55 millions. These estimates might reflect the possibly more sophisticated and integrated capital markets of Canada and the U.K. during the observation period. Or at least the estimates might imply this. Alternatively, they might reflect the fact that while the euro-dollar rate is a suitable representative overseas interest rate in the U.K. case, it is not in the French and German cases. However, it is not obvious why this should be so.

Another striking feature about the values for α is that they are all incompatible with the Cambist view that α should be some large if not infinite number because the covered interest arbitrage schedule should be perfectly elastic. Indeed, it is ironical that α is lowest in the French case since Cambism is very much a French school of financial thought. Apart from this incompatibility, the values for α are all quite low, indicating that covered-interest arbitrage is not very elastic.

The estimates of β are also quite low, especially in the French and West German cases. However, it should be recalled that the French and West German estimates were obtained indirectly from the spot market estimates for α which are lower than their forward market counterparts in Canada and the U.K. Despite this, the speculation schedules in the U.K. and Canada are relatively elastic. An implication of these observations would be that perceived exchange risk in the French and West German cases was relatively high and /or that speculators in these markets were more risk-averse.

Unfortunately there is only one estimate for γ. It is worth noting that the estimates for γ and β in the U.K. case are quite similar, suggesting that spot and forward speculation are as risky as each other, as might be expected.

The slopes of the long-term uncovered interest arbitrage schedules are reported. Here, the French and West German values for δ are considerably greater than the U.K. estimate, i.e. as compared with the short-term estimates the relative responses are reversed. There is no obvious explanation for this reversal other than the argument that the relative perceptions of risk are reversed.

We now turn to the determination of exchange-rate expectations. In particular we review the performance of equation 4.23, which was an application of the rational expectations hypothesis in the context of fixed exchange rates. In the last analysis all hypothesis-testing is relative; the rational expectations hypothesis can only be assessed in comparison with the performance of its principal competitors. No attempt has been made to do this in the present study although there is clearly a need for it. Ours has been the less ambitious objective of investigating whether or not the data are at least consistent with the rationality assumption.

However, one may accept the ideas behind equation 4.23 without necessarily accepting the normative implications of the rational expectations hypothesis as discussed in the first sections of Chapter 4, or what Laidler [1976, pp. 70–7] has called 'fully-blown rational expectations'. On the other hand, it would have been difficult to accept 'fully-blown rational expectations' had equation 4.23 been unsuccessful at the empirical level. In addition, there are a range of difficulties that arise when trying to test the rational expectations hypothesis, not least of which is the conceptual difficulty of what constitutes an adequate test. It is virtually impossible to know what the relevant model is. Even if there were agreement on the structure of the model there would still be ample scope for disagreement on the parameter values, lag structures, etc. A related complication is that speculators could be rational in different ways that reflected divergent perceptions about how the economy works. For example the 'monetarists' could be speculating against the 'Keynesians' while at the same time different sub-groups of 'monetarists' and 'Keynesians' respectively could be speculating against each other, because each considers the other has the wrong version of the truth.

Therefore, our course is to steer clear of these and related neo-medieval intellectual dilemmas. Instead, we interpret equation 4.23 as indicating that on the whole speculators look to the underlying economic causes of the future as opposed to acting on the basis of some arbitrary behavioural proposition.

Table 7.2 sets out the performance of equation 4.23 in the various equations for the various countries. A tick indicates a satisfactory performance of the variable and the absence of a tick indicates the opposite. The table distinguishes between the underlying variable such as relative prices (RXP) from the 'pressure' variable (VB).

TABLE 7.2   Performance of Rational Expectations Hypothesis

		UK	Canada	France	W.Germany
forward	RXP	$\checkmark$	$\checkmark^a$	$\checkmark$	$\checkmark$
rate	VB	$\checkmark$		$\checkmark$	$\checkmark^b$
short-term	RXP	$\checkmark$	n.a.	$\checkmark$	
capital	VB	$\checkmark$	n.a.	$\checkmark$	$\checkmark$
long-term	RXP	$\checkmark^c$	n.a.	$\checkmark$	
capital	VB	$\checkmark^c$	n.a.		

[a] from equation (6.6);   [b] ΔRES in equation 6.9;   [c] based on two equations.

Table 7.2 shows that a 'full house' was achieved in seven out of the eleven possible cases (Canada counts twice because of the two estimation periods) or eight out of twelve cases if the two U.K. equations on long-term capital flows are counted. 'Half houses' were achieved on nine out of eleven cases. The most impressive performance was achieved in relation to the forward rate equations and least impressive performance was with the equation for long-term capital flows. If anything, Table 7.2 suggests that equation 4.23 is less applicable in the context of long-term expectations where expectations might be generated in relation to a different range of criteria.

Turning now to the performance of equation 4.23 by country, a 'full house' is achieved in the U.K. case. The French case is also fairly impressive, but the German case is the least satisfactory. Given the relationship between the forward market and short-term capital flows one would expect a consistent generation mechanism for expectations between these two markets. This expectation is fulfilled in the British and French cases but is not fulfilled in the German case.

On the whole, Table 7.2 is fairly encouraging as these things go. In particular, the U.K. data are consistent with the rationality assumption across the full range of the capital account. When it is realised that in the longer run the most useful rational predictor of exchange rates in the purchasing power parity logic as summarised in equation 3.34i it may be relevant only to specify RXP in the long-term flows equations. In this case the French data would be compatible with the rationality assumption too.

Responses to Policy

In Table 7.3 are summarised the responses of the capital account to three main policy measures that might be expected in the light of the equations reported in this and the previous chapter. These responses are calculated under the *ceteris paribus* assumption especially regarding interest rates, the spot rate and exchange rate expectations. In practice none of these conditions are likely to be fulfilled, in which case the responses are likely to be smaller than those reported in Table 7.3.

The three policy measures are as follows:

(i) The authorities raise short-term interest rates by one annual percentage point while overseas interest rates remain unchanged.

(ii) The authorities raise long-term interest rates by one annual percentage point while long-term interest rates overseas remain unchanged.

(iii) The authorities buy 100 million units of their own currency forward.

The responses are expressed in both domestic currency and U.S. dollars (for purposes of international comparison) on the basis of the exchange rates at the foot of Table 7.1.

TABLE 7.3   Capital Account Responses to Policy Measures (millions)

	U.K. £	U.K. $	Canada[a] CAN$	Canada[a] $	France FF	France $	W. Germany DM	W. Germany $
(i)	64.5	154.8	105	105	31.5	5.7	22	5.5
			(212)			(12.2)		(11.7)
(ii)	180	432	n.a.	n.a.	6402	1164	9500	2375
(iii)[b]	94.5		98.2		88.2		96.8	

[a] Fixed rate period.   [b] Derived from the estimate of $\alpha/(\alpha + \beta)$: see equation (2.20).

A number of policy generalisations may be inferred from Table 7.3.

(i) The capital account is not very sensitive to domestic interest rate policy. In fact, it is highly insensitive to such policies. In the French and West German cases the insensitivity is especially pronounced due to a combination of inelastic covered arbitrage and forward speculation schedules. However, care should be taken in comparing the British with the other results since in the British case γ was separately estimated. If it is assumed that $\gamma = \beta$ as the U.K. results in Table 7.1 imply, the Canadian, French and West German responses would be the bracketed values, which still leaves France and West Germany well down on the list.

 (ii) In contrast, the long-term capital account is more interest-sensitive, especially in the cases of France and West Germany. What is most probably more important than the precise magnitudes here is the fact that in all cases the response at the long end is higher than the short end. These estimates at the very least suggest that the authorities' preoccupation with the effect of short-term interest rates on the capital account may have been misplaced. More assertively, they suggest that long-term interest rates might be a more useful weapon for influencing the capital account than the more traditional reliance on short-term money market policies. However, the effects of long-term interest rate policies are likely to take up to two or three years to be fully achieved. An additional issue is that the authorities might have less leverage over long-term interest rates than they have over short-term interest rates. Or that they can only influence long-term interest rates slowly whereas they can influence short-term interest rates fairly rapidly.

 (iii) Finally, the logic of the estimates imply that forward intervention is likely to have a very strong impact on the capital account. For example in the U.K. case, for every £100 of forward purchases of sterling, there is likely to be a spot inflow of £94.50. In the Canadian case there is a 98.2 per cent leverage from forward intervention on the spot market. This ratio is high because the speculative demand for forward exchange is inelastic relative to the covered arbitrage demand. Thus, when the authorities buy sterling forward it is taken up in the main by arbitrageurs who have to buy spot exchange in order to sell it forward to the authorities, rather than speculators who do not.

These estimates subsequently imply that forward intervention is a very powerful policy weapon for influencing the capital account. It is of course impossible to judge how far various monetary authorities have made use of this weapon since forward intervention data are not generally available. However, it may be the case that much of this power is lost when it is most needed. When there are speculative pressures on the balance of payments, official forward sales will be taken up in larger proportions by speculators i.e. the speculation schedule shifts, and the impact of the intervention on the spot market will be seriously reduced. Something of this nature happened during the sterling devaluation crisis in 1967 as is testified by the EEA's extensive forward market losses that were reported (in *Economic Trends*) during the early part of 1968. As a peacetime weapon, however, forward intervention could be quite effective even if it is recognised that its need during these times is unlikely to be very great.

8 The Term Structure of Forward Exchange Rates

While active trading takes place across a spectrum of forward exchange maturities previous theoretical (e.g. Branson [1968, Chapter 21]) and empirical work (e.g. Stoll [1968], Kesselman [1971]) has concentrated almost exclusively on the case of a single forward maturity. There have been some exceptions such as Grubel [1966, pp. 52–5] and Sohmen [1966, pp. 36–8]. However, Grubel no more than outlines the problem and Sohmen's main concern was the single maturity case. Porter [1971] has discussed how the term structure of international uncovered interest rate differentials might measure the implicit term structure of exchange rate expectations and Siegel [1972] describes how the term structure of forward rates might indicate the timing of future exchange rate developments. The existing literature on forward market activity and short-term capital movements has usefully been reviewed by Hodjera [1973].

Similarly, analyses of short-term capital movements in the spot exchange market, e.g. Hodjera [1971] have assumed a single maturity, e.g. the three-month covered differential, whereas in practice capital movements are likely to respond to an entire term structure of covered differentials. In the present chapter, therefore, an attempt is made at providing a theory of the determination of the term structure of forward exchange rates. It will be shown that a more general specification of maturities implies a richer set of theoretical possibilities than the conventional single maturity analysis and in some cases upsets previous theoretical conclusions.

In section A the single maturity framework of Branson [1968, Chapter 2] is used as a starting-point for a portfolio theoretic investigation of the micro-economics of the term structure of forward exchange rates. Section B presents a macro-economic analysis of the term structure of forward exchange rates where the relationship between various forward rates and exogenous variables is examined. Finally, in section C some tentative empirical results are reported of an econometric investigation of the three-month and twelve-month £/$ forward rates.

Attention will be focused exclusively on the partial equilibrium determination of the term structure of forward exchange rates. That is to say no attempt will be made at an analysis of the simultaneous determination of the term structure of forward rates and the term structure of international uncovered differentials. This term structure as well as the spot exchange rate are therefore assumed to be exogenous. A general equilibrium analysis would require separate treatment once the principles of the partial equilibrium analysis were understood.

However, there is at first sight a surprising disparity between the richness of the more familiar term structure of domestic interest rates where maturities extend beyond twenty years and the term structure of forward rates where active trading does not usually extend beyond the twelve month maturity which is the longest maturity published in the *Financial Times*. Even if a comparison is made, perhaps more appropriately, with the term structure of internationally traded financial assets, e.g. euro-dollars where active trading extends up to five years, a considerable disparity remains.

The reasons for this disparity are unclear. The financier who issues a twenty-year bond is implicitly assuming that this is cheaper subject to uncertainty considerations than issuing twenty one-year bonds or some other such combination. (See Telser [1967] for a useful survey of the literature on the term structure of domestic interest rates.) Similarly the investor who buys the bond is implicitly assuming that he will be at least as well off as if he bought twenty consecutive one-year bonds. Thus both sides of the bond market implicitly take very long views indeed about the future. In the forward markets twenty-year cover can only be obtained by twenty successive purchases of one-year cover or some similar combination despite the fact that the risk of issuing a twenty-year bond is, in principle, the same as the risk of entering into a twenty-year forward contract. However, in the absence of a better explanation, one is forced to conclude that in practice the risk of the latter is greater than the former risk, even to the extent of being prohibitive.

A more institutional approach might follow the argument that whereas market segmentation exists within the context of domestic financial assets the same institutional circumstances do not apply to the forward exchange markets. For example, within the confines of the market for domestic financial assets, the objective functions of life assurance companies and the pension funds in particular are such that these institutions prefer longer habitats as a means of avoiding capital uncertainty given the long-term nature of their liabilities, whereas other investors and institutions prefer shorter habitats. Were this not the case it is conceivable that the term structure of interest rates might be no more developed than the term structure of forward rates, with investors taking views over a twelve-month horizon on a wait-and-see basis. In the context of the forward exchange markets there are no special institutional factors which would make twenty-year forward contracts more attractive than a string of shorter-term contracts.

Both these considerations most probably go some way in explaining the relative narrowness of the maturity structure of the forward exchange markets in the absence of a more satisfactory explanation.

A. Micro-Economic Analysis

The analysis is presented in terms of two forward exchange maturities which represent the short-term and long-term forward rates respectively. As will be seen, by seeking to analyse the term structure of forward exchange rates one is immediately confronted by complexities which are absent in the single-maturity case and these complexities escalate with the number of maturities. Accordingly, the essence of the argument is presented in terms of two maturities only, which nevertheless presents enough complexities in its own right.

Portfolio Strategies

In this section, we consider the choices that confront an investor who is free to construct his portfolio in terms of domestic (D) and overseas assets (F) which can be long (L) or short-dated (S). Apart from the nationality of the asset and its maturity, the investor must also decide whether or not to cover forward any foreign positions that he buys. Thus we have two additional identifiers; C denotes a covered position and U an uncovered position. Conceptually, we can distinguish no less than twelve market strategies that face the investor over a holding period which is arbitrarily set at two periods, i.e. to coincide with the maturity of the long-dated bond and forward contract maturing at the end of the second period. In principle and in practice there will be n periods. These strategies are:

1. *LD*: i.e. hold domestic long-term bonds to maturity. The return on this strategy will be:

    $$Q_1(1 + RLD)$$

    where Q_1 is the amount invested in *LD* and R denotes the yield.

2. *SD.SD*: i.e. hold domestic short-dated bonds through to their maturity at the end of the first period and then in the second period purchase another short-dated domestic bond. The yield on this strategy will be:

    $$Q_2(1 + RSD)(1 + RSD^e)$$

    At the beginning of the first period the investor can of course only have an expectation of RSD in the second period, hence the specification of RSD^e. According to the neo-classical theory of the term structure

$$(1 + RSD)(1 + RSD^e) = (1 + RLD)$$

in which case the long-term rate is hypothesised to depend on expectations about the short-term rate.

3. *LFC*: i.e. the investor holds foreign long-term bonds to maturity on a covered basis which will yield

$$Q_3 \frac{XL}{Z1} \ (1 + RFL)$$

where $Z1$ is the spot rate at the beginning of the first period and XL is the long-term forward rate.

4. *LFU*: If the investor does not cover his position forward his expected yield on holding long term foreign bonds expressed in domestic currency will be:

$$Q_4 \frac{Z^e L}{Z1} \ (1 + RFL)$$

where $Z^e L$ is the expected value of the spot rate as conceived at the beginning of the first period with regard to the end of the second period.

5. *SFC.SFC*: i.e. he holds foreign short-term bonds in the first period on a covered basis and repeats this action in the second period. The expected yield on this position will be:

$$Q_5 \frac{XS}{Z1} \ (1 + RSF) \ \frac{XS^e}{Z^e} \ (1 + RSF^e)$$

where Z^e is the expected value of the spot rate as conceived at the beginning of the first period with regard to the beginning of the second period. Similarly XS^e is the expected value of the short-term forward rate and RSF^e the expected value of the short-term overseas interest rate.

6. *SFU.SFU*: This strategy is analogous to the previous one when positions are left uncovered. The expected yield in this case will be:

$$Q_6 \frac{Z^e}{Z1} \ (1 + RSF) \ \frac{Z^e L}{Z^e} \ (1 + RSF^e)$$

$$= \quad Q_6 \frac{Z^e L}{Z1} (1 + RSF) \ (1 + RSF^e)$$

which is of course the equivalent of staying in foreign currency until end of the second period.

7. *SFC.SFU*: i.e. covers in the first period but not in the second. The expected yield will then be:

$$Q_7 \frac{XS}{Z1} \ (1 + RSF) \ \frac{Z^e L}{Z^e} \ (1 + RSF^e)$$

8. *SFU.SFC*: or he might opt for the converse position, i.e. staying uncovered in the first period and covering only in the second, in which case the expected yield will be:

$$Q_8 \frac{Z^e}{Z1} \ (1 + RSF) \ \frac{XS^e}{Z^e} \ (1 + RSF^e)$$

$$= Q_8 \frac{XS^e}{Z1} \ (1 + RSF)(1 + RSF^e)$$

9. *SD.SFC*: In this case the investor holds short-term domestic bonds in the first period and short-term foreign bonds covered in the second period. The expected yield on this strategy will be:

$$Q_9(1 + RSD) \ \frac{XS^e}{Z^e} \ (1 + RSF^e)$$

10. *SFC.SD*: This is the counterpart to the previous case; the investor holds a short-term foreign position in the first period and holds short-term domestic bonds in the second, in which case the expected yield will be:

$$Q_{10} \frac{XS}{Z1} \ (1 + RSF)(1 + RSD^e)$$

11. *SD.SFU*: He holds domestic short-term bonds in the first period and uncovered foreign short-term bonds in the second. The expected yield will therefore be:

$$Q_{11}(1 + RSD) \ \frac{Z^e L}{Z^e} \ (1 + RSF^e)$$

12. *SFU.SD*: i.e. the counterparts to the previous case. The investor holds uncovered short-term bonds in the first period and holds domestic short-term bonds in the second. The expected yield on this strategy is expressed as:

$$Q_{12} \frac{Z^e}{Z1} \ (1 + RSF)(1 + RSD^e)$$

This completes the identification of all the strategies in the simplest of cases under review. The introduction of further maturities escalates the permutations into unmanageable proportions. In practice of course investors will implicitly weigh up all these strategies in the course of constructing some desirable portfolio. In what follows we discuss this simplest case.

Unfortunately, all twelve strategies are completely independent. For example, consider the following set of options:

SFC.SFC   SFU.SFU   SFC.SFU   SFU.SFC

Even if each option were additive rather than multiplicative, i.e. if instead of *SFC.SFC* we represented the expected yield as *SFC + SFC*, it would be impossible to find a combination of the first two options which satisfied some desired allocation between all four of the options despite the fact that the last two bear common terms with the first two.

Apart from default risk only two options are risk-free, namely options 1, *LD* and 3, *LFC*. However, even here the investor might have a preference for the relative liquidity of short-dated bonds given any uncertainties regarding his liquidity requirements over the holding period. Thus options 1 and 3 will contain an element of subjective uncertainty corresponding to the expected cost of encashing the bonds before they mature. In practice therefore the yields on all the strategies will have a density function.

The investor must generate expectations for no less than five variables; the domestic short-term bond rate, the foreign short-term bond rate, the spot rate at the end of the first and second periods and the short-term forward rate applicable to the second period. We shall assume these expectations and their respective density functions are given.

Portfolio Balance

For convenience, we shall represent the respective yields by the symbol Y so that for example in the case of the sixth strategy the expected yield is written as $Q_6 Y_6$. The expected return on the portfolio as a whole is therefore:

$$E(\pi) = \sum_{i=1}^{12} Q_i Y_i \tag{8.1}$$

and the expected variance of this return is:

$$\sigma^2(\pi) = \sum_{i=1}^{12} Q^2_i \sigma^2_i + 2 \sum_{j \neq i} Q_i Q_j \, \sigma_{ij} \tag{8.2}$$

where σ^2_i is the expected variance of Y_i and σ_{ij} is the expected covariance between Y_i and Y_j. The investor's net worth (W) is assumed to be a constraint on the total size of the portfolio so that:

$$\sum_{i=1}^{12} Q_i = W \tag{8.3}$$

and we assume that he seeks to maximise the expected utility on his portfolio given his desire to earn profits when averse to risk. The expected utility function has the standard properties of risk aversion:

$$E[U(\pi)] = H(\sigma^2(\pi), E(\pi)) \tag{8.4}$$

where $\partial H/\partial \sigma^2(\pi) = H^1{}_1 < 0$

$$\partial H/\partial E(\pi) = H^1{}_2 > 0$$

The lagrangean of this system is

$$L = H\left[\sum_{i=1}^{12} Q_i^2 \sigma_i^2 + 2\sum_{j \neq i} Q_i Q_j \sigma_{ij}, \sum_{i=1}^{12} Q_i Y_i\right] \\ - \lambda\left[\sum_{i=1}^{12} Q_i - W\right] \tag{8.5}$$

where λ is the lagrange multiplier.

This system has thirteen first-order conditions for a maximum:

$$\left.\begin{aligned}\frac{\partial L}{\partial Q_i} &= H^1{}_2 Y_i + 2H^1{}_1\Big(Q_i\sigma_i{}^2 + \sum_{j \neq i} Q_j\sigma_{ij}\Big) = \lambda \qquad \text{i} \\ &\quad (i = 1, 2, \ldots, 12) \\ \frac{\partial L}{\partial \lambda} &= \sum_{i=1}^{12} Q_i - W = 0 \qquad\qquad\qquad\qquad\quad \text{ii}\end{aligned}\right\} \tag{8.6}$$

which in matrix representation is expressed:

$$2H^1{}_1 \sum \mathbf{Q}^1 = -H^1{}_2 \mathbf{Y}^1 \tag{8.7}$$

where

$$\left.\begin{aligned}\sum &= \begin{bmatrix} 0 & \frac{1}{2}H^1{}_1 & \frac{1}{2}H^1{}_1 & \ldots\ldots & \frac{1}{2}H^1{}_1 \\ 1 & \sigma^2{}_1 & \sigma_{12} & \ldots\ldots & \sigma_{1\,12} \\ 1 & \sigma_{21} & \sigma_2{}^2 & \ldots\ldots & \sigma_{2\,12} \\ \cdot & \cdot & \cdot & & \cdot \\ \cdot & \cdot & \cdot & & \cdot \\ \cdot & \cdot & \cdot & & \cdot \\ 1 & \sigma_{12\,1} & \ldots\ldots\ldots\ldots\ldots & \sigma_{12}^2 \end{bmatrix} \quad \text{i.} \\ \mathbf{Q} &= (-\lambda/2H^1{}_1 \;\; Q_1 \;\; Q_2 \ldots\ldots Q_{12}) \qquad \text{ii} \\ \mathbf{Y} &= (W/H^1{}_2 \;\; Y_1 \;\; Y_2 \ldots\ldots Y_{12}) \qquad\quad \text{iii}\end{aligned}\right\} \tag{8.8}$$

Thus the equilibrium portfolio is:

$$\mathbf{Q}^{1*} = \frac{-H^1{}_2}{2H^1{}_1} \sum{}^{-1} \mathbf{Y} \tag{8.9}$$

It is clear that even for the simplest of cases where there are only two maturities the evaluation of $\sum^{-1}\mathbf{Y}^1$ becomes very complex indeed. However, to demonstrate the general nature of the asset demand functions implied by this equilibrium portfolio we simplify the analysis by assuming that the investor is faced with only three strategies. The equilibrium value of say the first asset would be:

$$Q_1^* = \frac{-H^1_2}{det\,\Sigma_3\,4(H^1_1)^2} \left[\; Y_1(\sigma_2^2 + \sigma_3^2 - 2\sigma_{23}) \right.$$

$$- Y_2(\sigma_{12} + \sigma_3^2 - \sigma_{32} - \sigma_{13}) + Y_3(\sigma_{32} + \sigma_{12} - \sigma_2^2 - \sigma_{13})$$

$$- W/H^1_2(\sigma_{12}(\sigma_3^2 - \sigma_{23}) - \sigma_2^2(\sigma_3^2 - \sigma_{13})$$

$$\left. + \sigma_{32}(\sigma_{23} - \sigma_{13})) \right] \tag{8.10}$$

If $det\,\Sigma_3 > 0$, then for $\dfrac{\partial Q_1}{\partial Y_1} > 0$ it is necessary that $2\sigma_{23} > \sigma_2^2 + \sigma_3^2$.

Similarly for competing rates to have the usual negative effect, it is necessary that

$$\sigma_{32} + \sigma_{13} > \sigma_{12} + \sigma_3^2$$

and $\quad\;\; \sigma_{32} + \sigma_{12} > \sigma_2^2 + \sigma_{13}$

For the wealth effect to be positive it will be necessary that

$$\sigma_{12}(\sigma_3^2 - \sigma_{23}) + \sigma_{32}(\sigma_{23} - \sigma_{13}) > \sigma_2^2(\sigma_3^2 - \sigma_{13})$$

If the constellations of the bordered variance-covariance matrix is such that $det\,\Sigma_3 < 0$ then these conditions will have to be reversed for the demand elasticities to have the appropriate sign. One conclusion that can be reached from this analysis is that the expected yield on a particular strategy can rise but that this produces a negative effect on the equilibrium holding of the strategy. In practice, however, this is unlikely. Another implication of the analysis is that asset demand functions are non-linear in the variance and covariances of the yields of the various strategies. This is of particular importance with regard to econometric investigation of these asset demand functions where complex non-linearities of this form are most probably difficult to deal with. It will also be noticed that many of the yields of the alternative strategies have common terms. In practice therefore, it might be possible to sign some of the elements in the Σ matrix.

Pure Speculative Demand

In the previous section we considered the allocation of funds among a number of alternative strategies. Some of these strategies involved the assumption of uncovered positions with regard to exchange risk, in which case forward market speculation is implicit in the analysis. However, in principle forward exchange speculation need not be constrained by the quantity of net funds to be allocated since the purchase of forward contracts does not require any spot positions. In practice, aversion to risk would act as a constraint on the size of the forward contract to which an investor is prepared to commit himself. In this section we discuss pure forward market speculation when there are multiple maturities.

It should be noted that all investors must behave as speculators in a wider sense since in principle there is no yield which is not a random variable in the sense of the previous section. For example, even strategies 1 and 3 would incorporate random variables in the general case of an infinite horizon even if they do not under the clearly artificial and heuristic context of the two-period horizon. In practice, therefore, in addition to default risks all yields would be random variables with investors having to take views not only about future spot rates, but also about future forward rates and future interest rates at home and abroad.

We now return to the question of pure speculation. The pure speculator is confronted by only two strategies when the scenario of the previous section is assumed to prevail:

> i.   He can speculate by contracting in the short-term forward market in the first period, followed by another short-term contract in the second. The expected return on the first period contract is $Q_1(XS - Z^e)$ where Q_1 represents the size of the contract. This is the difference between the forward price at which the contract is purchased and the spot price that is expected on the date of maturity of this contract.
> Q_1 can be positive or negative depending on whether the speculator holds foreign or domestic currency forward. The expected return in the second period will be:
>
> $$Q_2(XS^e - Z^e L)$$
>
> ii.   If the speculator holds long-term forward contracts his expected return will be $Q_3(XL - Z^e L)$, i.e. the difference between the long-term forward rate and the spot rate that is expected to prevail when these long-term forward contracts mature. Following the previous notation we have:
>
> $$E(\pi) = \sum_{i=1}^{3} Q_1 Y_i \qquad (8.11)$$

and $\qquad \sigma^2(\pi) = \sum_{i=1}^{3} \left[\sigma_i^2 Q_i^2 + 2 \sum_{j \neq i} Q_i Q_j \sigma_{ij} \right] \qquad (8.12)$

The equilibrium portfolio solution will be of the same form as the case where net wealth was constrained, although of course Σ will not be bordered and Y and Q will exclude W and $-\lambda$ respectively. The solution for Q_1 will imply the speculative demand for the short-term forward contracts and that for Q_3, the speculative demand for long-term contracts. For example:

$$Q^*_1 = \frac{-H^1_2}{2\,det\,\Sigma\,H^1_1}(\sigma_2^2\sigma_3^2 - \sigma^2_{32})(XS - Z^e)$$

$$-(\sigma_{12}\sigma_3^2 - \sigma_{13}\sigma_{32})(XS^e - Z^e L)$$

$$-(\sigma_2{}^2\sigma_{13} - \sigma_{12}\sigma_{23})(XL - Z^e L)) \tag{8.13}$$

is the demand function for short-term contracts. If $det\,\Sigma$ is positive the normal pattern of demand responses would require

$$\left.\begin{array}{ll} \sigma_2{}^2\sigma_3{}^2 > \sigma_{32}{}^2 & \text{i} \\[2mm] \sigma_2{}^2\sigma_{13} > \sigma_{12}\sigma_{23} & \text{ii} \end{array}\right\} \tag{8.14}$$

These conditions would once again have to be reversed if $det\,\Sigma$ happened to be negative.

B. Macro-Economic Analysis

Aggregation

So far we have been considering the behaviour of the typical investor who is confronted by a set of alternative market strategies and a set of objective market yields. The investor is analogous to the firm in perfect competition who is a price taker rather than a price maker. In the present section, we analyse how objective market yields, particularly the term structure of forward rates, is determined within the 'industry' setting, i.e. when aggregating across individual portfolios. In what follows we assume that expectations of random variables are predetermined and more heroically still we assume that domestic and foreign interest rates and the spot exchange rate are given. Our purpose is therefore to concentrate on the determination of the structure of forward rates.

Strategies 5, 7 and 10 involve the purchase of short-term forward contracts in domestic currency. Thus in principle the aggregate demand function for short-term forward contracts in domestic currency is obtained according to the following stages:

    i.   Derive Q^*_{ij} ($i = 5, 7, 10$), i.e. determine the desired strategy mix for the jth ($j = 1, 2, \ldots, J$) portfolio agent where short-term forward contracts are complements to these strategies.

    ii.   Derive HS_j where HS is the net demand for short-term forward contracts in domestic currency.

    iii. Derive $\sum_{j=1}^{J} HS_j$ for the excess demand for short-term forward contract for the market as a whole.

To simplify the aggregation process the results of the micro-economic investigation are linearised both with respect to the parameters in the various asset demand functions and with respect to the component parts of the yields on the different strategies. The former assumption implies that Σ is fixed over time, the second implies that the component yields are expressed in logarithmic form. Out of all the market strategies there are twelve component yields and prices, objective and subjective. In what follows subscripts on the parameter a denote how these particular components determine the demand for short-term forward contracts through the respective strategies. Thus $-a_1 RLD$ means that increases in domestic long-term rates depress the demand for short-term forward contracts in domestic currency terms via their effect on the demand for the first strategy. Thus:

$$
\begin{aligned}
HS = {} & -a_1 RLD - RSD(a_2 + a_9 + a_{11}) - RSD^e(a_2 - a_{10} + a_{12}) \\
& - a_3 XL - RLF(a_3 + a_4) - Z^e L(a_4 + a_6 - a_7 + a_{11}) \\
& + Z1(a_3 + a_4 - a_5 + a_6 - a_7 + a_8 - a_{10} + a_{12}) \\
& + XS(a_5 + a_7 + a_{10}) + RSF(a_5 - a_6 + a_7 - a_8 + a_{10} - a_{12}) \\
& + XS^e(a_5 - a_8 - a_9) - Z^e(a_5 + a_7 - a_9 - a_{11} + a_{12}) \\
& + RSF^e(a_5 - a_6 + a_7 - a_8 - a_9 - a_{11})
\end{aligned}
\tag{8.15}
$$

It will be noticed that only five out of the twelve coefficients in this demand function are of determinate sign. For example, we can conclude that an increase in the domestic short-term bond rate will reduce the demand for short term forward contracts in domestic currency since strategies 2, 9, and 11 compete with strategies 5, 7 and 10. If the cost of short-term forward contracts falls in terms of foreign currency, i.e. if XS rises the demand for HS will rise through strategies 5, 7 and 10. Conversely if the cost of long-term forward contracts falls, i.e. if XL rises the demand for HS falls via strategy 3, and if the long-term foreign bond rate rises the demand for HS falls through strategies 3 and 4.

However, more than half of the coefficients are of indeterminate sign on *a priori* grounds. It will be noticed for example that an increase in the short-term foreign bond rate raises the demand for HS through strategies 5, 7 and 10, i.e. the strategies in which short-term forward contracts in domestic currency and short-term foreign bonds are complementary; and lowers the demand for HS through strategies 6, 8 and 12, i.e. strategies which compete with strategies 5, 7 and 10. Thus whether a rise in short-term foreign bond rates will increase or decrease the demand for HS cannot be determined on an *a priori* basis. Yet there has been an overwhelming presumption in the literature that an increase in say the three-month foreign interest rate will raise the demand for three-month forward contracts in domestic currency. Another presumption has been that an increase in the spot rate (i.e. if $Z1$ falls) would tend to raise the demand for HS. Thus if domestic currency appreciates, the demand for forward domestic currency contracts rises through the covered-interest arbitrage mechanism. The present analysis demonstrates that this is true as far as strategies 5, 7 and 10 are concerned but false as far as strategies 3, 4, 6, 8 and 12 are concerned; the strategies which compete with 5, 7 and 10. Yet another presumption has been that if domestic currency is expected to appreciate (i.e. if Z^e falls) the market will tend to buy short-term forward contracts in domestic currency with the intention of selling the proceeds in the spot market on maturity. The present analysis once again shows that this is so as far as strategies 5, 7 and 12 are concerned but false as far as strategies 9 and 11 are concerned.

The difference between the standard analysis and the present schema is that the former has considered the case of a single forward maturity which left only three strategies from which the investor might select his portfolio.

   i. Investing in domestic bonds.
   ii. Investing in foreign bonds covered.
   iii. Investing in foreign bonds uncovered.

By doubling the maturities we quadruple the strategies, so it is not surprising that the analytical results that follow from the single-maturity case do not carry over to the multiple-maturity situation.

Let us now turn to the excess demand function for long-term forward contracts in domestic currency (HL) which is derived in an analogous fashion to HS, i.e. through the same portfolio framework and b plays the analogous role to a of denoting how the components of the yields of the various strategies affect HL. We find that:

$$
\begin{aligned}
HL ={}& b_1 RLD - RSD(b_2 + b_9 + b_{11}) - RSD^e(b_2 + b_{10} + b_{12}) \\
&+ b_3 XL - RLF(b_4 - b_3) - Z^e L(b_4 + b_6 + b_7 + b_{11}) \\
&- Z1(b_3 - b_4 - b_5 - b_6 - b_7 - b_8 - b_{10} - b_{11}) \\
&- XS(b_5 + b_7 + b_{10}) - RSF(b_5 + b_6 + b_7 + b_8 + b_{12}) \\
&- XS^e(b_5 + b_9 + b_8) + Z^e(b_5 + b_7 + b_9 + b_{11} + b_{12}) \\
&- RSF^e(b_5 + b_6 + b_7 + b_8 + b_9 + b_{10} + b_{11}) \qquad (8.16)
\end{aligned}
$$

In this case it will be noticed that nine out of the twelve coefficients are of determinate sign and that the coefficient of $Z1$ and Z^e are almost determinate. Only the coefficient on RLF is truly indeterminate; in strategy 3 an increase in the long-term foreign bond rate raises the demand for HL, but decreases it in the case of strategy 4. According to the standard single-maturity analysis only b_3 would have been considered.

It should of course be pointed out that the determinacy of so many of the coefficients in the HL equation and the indeterminacy of so many in the HS equation is largely spurious. By introducing a third maturity into the analysis we would have discovered that while the coefficients that in the two-maturities case are determinate would have remained determinate, there would be a whole range of new variables, e.g. RLF^e etc., whose coefficients in the three-maturities case would be indeterminate, just in the same way that RSF, while determinate in the single-maturity case, becomes indeterminate when there is more than one maturity. We would also have discovered that in the equation for HL, i.e. the demand for forward contracts in domestic currency in the third maturity, the majority of the coefficients would have been of determinate sign, as indeed they were in the case of HL when there were only two maturities in the analysis.

In principle, of course, there is an entire spectrum of maturities, in which case to select any two is arbitrary. In practice, however, the number of maturities might be limited and 'bunched', i.e. the majority of market activity might gravitate towards certain maturities. We have already pointed out that the forward exchange markets have a relatively restricted maturity structure, so that if we assume that trading is bunched at say around the three-month and twelve-month maturities a double maturity model might not be too unreasonable an approximation of the market as a whole.

Qualitative Analysis

So much for the derivation and specification of the market excess demand functions for short and long-term forward contracts in domestic currency. Equilibrium in the short-term market will exist when:

$$HS + GS = 0 \tag{8.17}$$

where GS represents the authorities' position in short-term forward exchange. Rewriting the coefficients in the equation for HS as A_i, this implies that the equilibrium short-term forward rate is given by:

$$XS = \frac{1}{A_8}(A_1 RLD + A_2 RSD + A_3 RSD^e + A_4 XL + A_5 RLF$$
$$+ A_6 Z^e L - A_6 Z1 - A_9 RSF - A_{10} XS^e + A_{11} Z^e$$
$$- A_{12} RSF^e - GS + A_{13} W) \tag{8.18}$$

where A_{13} is the implied coefficient on the net wealth variable. It will be noticed that because of the GS variable all the individual A_i coefficients are identified in the econometric sense. In other words the authorities' forward position is a most useful identifying restriction in a real world where unfortunately there is no information on HS, as has already been observed in Chapter 6.

Similarly equilibrium in the long-term forward market will obtain when:

$$HL + GL = 0 \tag{8.19}$$

where GL is the authorities' position in the long-term forward market. The equilibrium long-term forward rate will therefore be:

$$XL = \frac{1}{B_3}(B_1 RLD + B_2 RSD + B_4 RSD^e + B_5 RLF + B_6 Z^e L$$

$$+ B_7 Z + B_8 XS + B_9 RSF + B_{10} XS^e - B_{11} Z^e$$

$$+ B_{12} RSF^e - GL + B_{13} W) \tag{8.20}$$

where once again the absence of information on HL does not prevent the full identification of all the individual B_i coefficients provided that information is available on the authorities' long-term forward position.

We may not examine how the term structure of forward rates responds to changes in interest rates, market expectations and the authorities' forward positions at the short and the long-term maturities. Since our major concern is to concentrate the discussion on the determination of the term structure we assume that the spot rate $Z1$ is predetermined. The only endogenous variables, therefore, are the two forward rates XS and XL. The two-equation system in XS and XL can be written as:

$$\begin{bmatrix} 1 & -\dfrac{A_4}{A_8} \\[2ex] \dfrac{-B_8}{B_3} & 1 \end{bmatrix} \begin{bmatrix} XS \\[2ex] XL \end{bmatrix} = \begin{bmatrix} \dfrac{1}{A_8}\sum_i A_i z_i \\[2ex] \dfrac{1}{B_3}\sum_i B_i z_i \end{bmatrix} \tag{8.21}$$

where e.g. $z_i = RLD$ etc.

The determinant of the system is:

$$1 - \frac{A_4 B_8}{B_3 A_8} \equiv D \tag{8.22}$$

whose sign is indeterminate. However, using Samuelson's Correspondence Principle a necessary condition for stability is:

$$\frac{A_4 B_8}{A_8 B_3} < 1 \tag{8.23}$$

in which case the determinant will be positive, i.e. $D > 0$. We are now in a position to analyse the effects on the respective forward rates caused by changes in the predetermined variables.

  i.   GS increases:i.e. the authorities increase their short-term forward position in domestic currency. The total derivative of the system gives:

$$\frac{dXS}{dGS} = -\frac{1}{DA_8} < 0 \tag{8.24}$$

$$\frac{dXL}{dGS} = - \frac{B_8}{DA_8 B_3} < 0 \qquad (8.25)$$

i.e. both the short and long-term forward rates rise when the authorities increase their short-term forward position. In principle the response at the long end could be greater than the short-term response if:

$$\frac{B_8}{B_3} > 1$$

ii.   GL increases: i.e. the authorities increase their long-term forward position in domestic currency:

$$\frac{dXS}{dGL} = - \frac{A_4}{A_8 B_3 D} < 0 \qquad (8.26)$$

$$\frac{dXL}{dGL} = - \frac{1}{DB_3} < 0 \qquad (8.27)$$

i.e. both the short and long-term forward rates rise when the authorities increase their long-term forward position. The response at the short end would be greater than the response at the long end if:

$$\frac{A_4}{A_8} > 1$$

However, for stability if $\dfrac{A_4}{A_8} > 1$ then

$$\frac{B_3}{B_8} > \frac{A_4}{A_8}$$

iii.   RSD increases: e.g. if the authorities raise short-term domestic interest rates:

$$\frac{dXS}{dRSD} = \frac{1}{DA_8} \left(\frac{A_2 + A_4 B_2}{B_3} \right) > 0 \qquad (8.28)$$

$$\frac{dXL}{dRSD} = \frac{1}{DB_3} \left(\frac{B_2 + B_8 A_2}{A_8} \right) > 0 \qquad (8.29)$$

i.e. the foreign currency price of both short and long-term forward contracts of domestic currency falls when domestic interest rates rise. The short-term response occurs since short-term bonds always compete with strategies that involve short-term forward contracts and because long-term contracts always compete with short-term contracts. A similar reason accounts for the relationship at the long end.

iv.   *RLD* increases: if the authorities raise long-term interest rates then:

$$\frac{dXS}{dRLD} = \frac{1}{DA_8} \left(A_1 + \frac{B_1 A_4}{B_3} \right) > 0 \qquad (8.30)$$

$$\frac{dXL}{dRLD} = \frac{1}{DB_3} \left(B_1 + \frac{A_1 B_8}{A_8} \right) > 0 \qquad (8.31)$$

i.e. both forward rates fall because long-term bonds are always unambiguous competitors of strategies in which short and long-term forward contracts in domestic currency are involved.

v.   *RSF* increases: if short-term foreign bond rates rise then:

$$\frac{dXS}{dRSF} = \frac{1}{DA_8} \left(\frac{A_4 B_9}{B_3} - A_9 \right) \gtrless 0 \qquad (8.32)$$

$$\frac{dXL}{dRSF} = \frac{1}{DB_3} \left(B_9 - \frac{A_9 B_8}{A_8} \right) \lessgtr 0 \qquad (8.33)$$

i.e. the effects are indeterminate since the sign of A_9 is indeterminate. It is generally thought that an increase in the short-term bond rate overseas raises the demand for short-term forward contracts and therefore lowers XS. This implies that not only is $A_9 > 0$ but also:

$$A_9 > \frac{A_4 B_9}{B_3}$$

These indeterminacies occur whenever forward contracts are both complements and substitutes for the asset whose yield either objective or subjective is changing.

vi.   *RLF* increases: if long-term bond rates rise overseas the effect on forward rates is once again indeterminate because the sign of B_5 is indeterminate. Thus:

$$\frac{dXS}{dRLF} = \frac{1}{DA_8} \left(A_5 + \frac{B_5 A_4}{B_3} \right) \lessgtr 0 \qquad (8.34)$$

$$\frac{dXL}{dRLF} = \frac{1}{DB_3} \left(B_5 + \frac{A_5 B_8}{A_8} \right) \gtrless 0 \qquad (8.35)$$

Once again it is generally thought that an increase in long-term bond yields overseas raises the price of long-term forward contracts in domestic currency, i.e. $dXL/dRLF < 0$. For this to occur it is necessary that $B_5 < 0$ (i.e. $b_3 > b_4$) and that

$$B_5 + \frac{A_5 B_8}{A_8} \; < \; 0$$

Other analyses could be provided, however, the effects of the remaining predetermined variables on this simplified term structure of forward rates are indeterminate because forward contracts in domestic currency are both complements and substitutes with regard to the strategies in which the various yields occur. To the extent that they compete, the sign is determinate and is as generally indicated in the literature. To the extent that they are complementary the sign becomes indeterminate. The precise result then becomes empirical.

C. Empirical Analysis

The market clearing equations which have been described and which determine the short and long-term forward rates contain a large number of explanatory variables, many of which cannot be observed. To provide econometric proxies for a vector of domestic and overseas interest rate expectations at the long and short ends as well as vectors of expected exchange rates and forward rates would be impractical in the present context. Therefore, in what follows, a simplified model is suggested for which some tentative econometric estimates are provided. These results are intended to be illustrative of the problems that might be encountered in this area rather than corroboration for any particular view of the determination of the term structure of forward exchange rates.

The Simplified Model

We assume that short and long-term covered positions are substitutes for each other. Therefore, when the short-term covered differential improves because of a rise in, say, the domestic short-term interest rate the demand for domestic covered positions will rise for two reasons. First, international arbitrage would tend to attract short-term capital inflows, i.e. the familiar assumption of the conventional literature. Secondly, there will be substitution effects out of long-term covered positions. Short-term forward sales of domestic currency would subsequently be increased on both these counts. But long-term net sales would tend to fall.

In other words we assume away the ambiguities that have been identified, where it will be recalled that precisely this particular experiment had an ambiguous effect on the short and long-term forward rates. Alternatively, what we are seeking to do is to check the importance of ignoring such ambiguities.

Similarly the speculative demand for short-term forward exchange depends absolutely on the expected profitability of short-term speculation. This assumption accords with the previous analysis on pure speculation but once again ignores ambiguities outstanding from the analysis of the alternative strategies.

For the sake of linearisation we reintroduce the notation discussed in relation to equation 6.5. Thus all spot and forward rates are expressed as annualised percentage deviations from parity. The short-term forward rate is FS and the long-term forward rate is FL. Notice that whereas in the earlier parts of this chapter the exchange rate was expressed in terms of the amount of domestic currency required to buy a unit of foreign currency, henceforth this ratio is reversed.

The market for short-term forward exchange will be in equilibrium when:

$$- \alpha_1 (RSD - S + FS - RSF) - \alpha_2 (RSD + FS - RLD - FL)$$
$$- \alpha_3 (RSD + FS - S - RLF) + \beta_1 (S^e S - FS) + \beta_2 (S^e S - FS$$
$$- S^e L + FL) + GS = 0 \qquad (8.36)$$

where $\alpha_1 (\quad)$ is the arbitrage demand between domestic and overseas short-term positions, $\alpha_2 (\quad)$ is the arbitrage demand between covered short and covered long-term positions and $\alpha_3 (\quad)$ is the arbitrage demand between covered domestic short-term positions and overseas long-term positions. In this simple model all these demand functions do not incorporate any exchange risk. The speculative demand for domestic currency forward will depend on the expected profitability on short-term speculation $\beta_1 (\quad)$ and on the relative profitability between short and long-term forward market speculation (β_2).

Solving this equation for the short-term forward rate yields a simplified version of equation 8.18:

$$FS = \frac{1}{\alpha + \beta} \left[\alpha_1 (RSF - RSD - S) + \alpha_2 (RLD + FL - RSD) + \right.$$
$$\alpha_3 (RLF + S - RSD) + (\beta_1 + \beta_2) S^e S - \beta_2 (S^e L - FL) + GS$$
$$(8.37)$$

where $\alpha + \beta = \alpha_1 + \alpha_2 + \alpha_3 + \beta_1 + \beta_2$

i.e. the short-term forward rate varies inversely with domestic short-term interest rates and long-term exchange rate expectations and directly with both overseas interest rates, the long-term forward rate, the short-term expected spot rate and the official short-term forward position. Notice that the coefficient on GS econometrically identifies all the structural parameters of the model i.e. as in equation 3.15.

The analogous equation for the long-term forward rate would be:

$$FL = \frac{1}{\alpha_1^1 + \alpha_2 + \alpha_3^1 + \beta_1^1 + \beta_2} \left[\alpha_1^1 (RLF - RLD - S) + \right.$$

$$+ \alpha_2 (RSD + FS - RLD)$$

$$+ \alpha_3^1 (RSF + S - RLD)$$

$$+ (\beta_1^1 + \beta_2) S^e L - \beta_2 (S^e S - FS)$$

$$\left. + GL \right] \qquad (8.38)$$

where the causal principles are of course identical to those of the equation for FS. Notice that both equations include α_2 and β_2 since substitution effects between the two markets are naturally the same in both equations, and e.g. α_1^1 is the parameter on $(RLD - S + FL - RSF)$, the long-term covered differential.

The £/$ Term Structure

Attempts were made at estimating these equations using £/$ data where the short-term forward rate was proxied by the three-month rate and the long-term forward rate was proxied by the twelve-month forward rate. The equations were fitted using quarterly data over the period 1966 Q1– 1974 Q2. The following data were used:

RSD : three-month local authority deposit rate in U.K. (source: *Financial Statistics*, C.S.O., London).

RLD : twelve-month local authority deposit rate in U.K. (source: unpublished Bank of England. Also available in the *Financial Times*).

RSF : three-month euro-dollar deposit rate (source: *Bank of England Quarterly Bulletin*)

RLF : twelve-month euro-dollar deposit rate (source: Morgan Guaranty *Reports*. Also available in the *Financial Times*).

S : £/$ spot rate (source: *Bank of England Quarterly Bulletin*).

FS : £/$ three-month forward rate (source: *Bank of England Quarterly Bulletin*).

FL : £/$ twelve-month forward rate (source: Bank of England unpublished. Also available in the *Financial Times*).

S and FS are defined as in equation 6.5. However, the twelve-month forward rate has to be expressed as:

$$FL = \frac{(\text{forward rate} - \text{parity}) \; 100}{\text{parity}}$$

since we are concerned with annualised percentages. Also in the context of twelve-month differentials it is necessary to divide S for similar reasons by 4. All the above data are expressed as averages of end-month observations.

The expected spot rate is generated through the assumption phat the spot rate eventually adjusts to restore purchasing power parity in traded goods. This implies that the expected spot rate depends on a moving average of relative export prices, (RXP) i.e. as in Chapters 6 and 7. In practice, however, it would be very difficult to distinguish between the short and long-term expected spot rates from the point of view of econometric modelling. Therefore, a distributed lag on RXP is used to proxy:

$$\frac{\beta_2}{\alpha + \beta} \ [S^e S - S^e L]$$

As before, the Almon procedure was used for estimating this distributed lag and the simultaneity of spot and forward rates was treated by wayof instrumental variables.

Estimation was particularly difficult on account of the inevitable collinearity between the explanatory variables and on the whole the results were not encouraging. Nevertheless two equations are reported, one for the three-month forward rate and the other for the twelve-month rate.

$$FS_t = 11.6 - 0.737(RSD - RSF - \hat{S})_t - 0.167(RLF$$
$$(3.3) \qquad\qquad (0.75)$$
$$+ RLD + \hat{S})_t + 1.0152\,\hat{FL}_t + \sum_{i=0}^{14} w_i\,RXP_{t-i} \qquad (8.39)$$
$$(6.25)$$
$$R^2 = 0.959 \qquad \sigma = 0.8 \qquad DW = 1.3$$

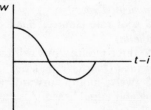

$$FL_t = -2.9 - 0.8636(RLD - RLF - \hat{S}/4)_t$$
$$(70.8)$$
$$- 0.741\,(RSF - RSD + \hat{FS} + \hat{S})_t + \sum_{i=0}^{16} v_i\,RXP_{t-i} \qquad (8.40)$$
$$(14.0)$$

$$R^2 = 0.995 \qquad \sigma = 0.349 \qquad DW = 1.77$$

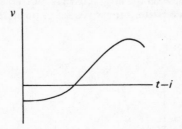

Neither of these equations conforms with the theoretical derivation since this was unfortunately the only way of obtaining results that were statistically satisfactory. However, in equation 8.39 the following coefficients cohere with the theoretical specification:

$$\frac{\alpha_1}{\alpha + \beta} = 0.737$$

$$\frac{\alpha_2 + \beta_2}{\alpha + \beta} = 1.0152$$

The latter coefficient implies that the short-term forward rate is dominated by substitution effects from the long-term forward market i.e. that $\alpha_1 + \alpha_3 + \beta_1$ are small relative to $\alpha_2 + \beta_2$. Both coefficients imply that $\alpha_2 + \beta_2 > \alpha_1$, which at least is consistent with this conclusion. Because of the high collinearity between RSD and RLD the coefficient of 0.167 most probably is an estimate of $\alpha_3/(\alpha + \beta)$, which once again points to the consistent conclusion that α_3 is relatively small. In other words, if anything, equation 8.39 implies that the two forward markets are highly integrated.

Equation 8.40 is even less informative. Only the coefficient of 0.8636 relates to the theoretical derivation. The coefficient of 0.741 indicates that changes in the three-month covered differential have a high feedback on to the twelve-month market, suggesting once more the high degree of substitution that takes place between the two markets.

The estimated lag structures on RXP are not individually reported because they were insignificant; only their shapes are provided graphically. Nevertheless, their shape is interesting since they accord with *a priori* expectations. The relationship between the expected spot rate and lagged value of RXP is likely to be described by a negative hump since an increase in U.K. export prices must eventually be matched by a depreciation of sterling. The curve marked 3 describes the lag structure with regard to the short-term expectation. The long-term expectation would therefore be related to RXP through the lag structure marked 12, since an observation at say t-k would be obsolescent for the more remote future although it might still be relevant for developments in the nearer term. In the equation 8.39 the latter curve is subtracted from the former curve and the implied pattern for w is a set of positive weights followed

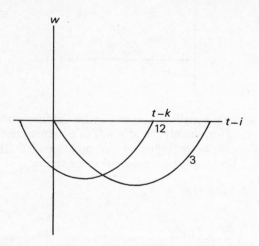

by a set of negative weights—which is in fact what was estimated. With equation 8.40 these arguments are reserved, in which case the vs should be initially negative and then eventually positive—which accords with the estimation.

Concluding Remarks

Clearly much more work remains to be done in this virgin territory. Apart from the empirical determinants of the term structure of forward exchange rates, it remains to be seen whether equations for capital movements may be improved by specifying multiple interest rate differentials. The preliminary results reported in equation 8.39 and 8.40 suggest that the three and twelve-month forward markets are closely integrated. If there were no segmentation at all between these markets, nothing would be lost by ignoring multiple maturities in conventional econometric investigation of capital movements.

9 The Euro-dollar Market

International financial transactions may occur either directly between two countries or indirectly via the international currency markets. In this chapter the euro-dollar market is taken as a representative international currency market to explore some theoretical and empirical relationships between the international currency markets and different domestic money markets. We begin by describing a theoretical model wherein the domestic interest rates of different national money markets are determined simultaneously with the euro-dollar rate in terms of both the direct and indirect international financial transactions that might typically occur. This model may be used as a theoretical basis for investigating the international financial interdependence of different currency areas in the presence of the intermediating influences of international currency markets.

Some empirical results on the determination of the euro-dollar rate are presented, drawing on the earlier theoretical discussion. In particular we attempt to establish the relative influence of U.S. and world money market conditions on the euro-dollar rate.

Whereas in Chapters 6 and 7 the approach was bilateral in so far as capital flows and forward rates were based on bilateral interest rate differentials, e.g. the differential between domestic interest rates and a single competing overseas rate, the approach in this chapter is multilateral in that the financial sectors of the U.K., France, Canada, W. Germany and the U.S. are linked via the euro-dollar market as an example of an international currency market.

Indeed this approach could form the basis of a world international payments model, the capital account analogue of the more familiar world trade models as developed, e.g., by Adams *et al* [1969], Samuelson [1974] and Beenstock and Minford [1976]. For example, if say French interest rates rose, this would influence the euro-dollar rate via the mechanism to be described in this chapter. The euro-dollar rate would thus influence the capital accounts of the countries that were party to the world payments model via the kind of equations already discussed in Chapter 6 and 7. This in turn would feed into the monetary sectors of those countries, which would affect their interest rates. Finally, these interest-rate changes would affect the euro-dollar rate again and a second iteration would be launched.

This approach to world monetary modelling is of course only an approximation to a correct specification where all monetary sectors of different countries would be simultaneously interrelated. However, this specification would raise some formidable econometric hurdles. The alternative two-tier approach suggested here of first estimating bilateral capital account models in terms of competing internationally traded assets and then developing a simple multilateral model to link the models in the first stage has an appeal both regarding practicality and some elegance. In addition it may be a reasonable approximation to an ideal specification.

Just in the same way as the euro-dollar market has developed at the short end of the maturity structure (for a description and historical analysis see Clendenning [1971] and Bell [1973]), so in the very recent past the euro-bond market has been emerging as an international market regarding longer maturities. Indeed, the theoretical and empirical analysis in this chapter would be applicable to an investigation of the euro-bond market too. In other words, a multilateral empirical analysis of the euro-dollar rate could link the short-term capital accounts in the two-tier approach to world monetary modelling, and a multilateral empirical analysis of the euro-bond rate could serve to link the long-term capital accounts.

All this is by way of suggestion for future research in this relatively unexplored area; no attempts to construct such a model are reported here. We turn now to some theoretical considerations regarding the monetary linkages that are implied by the existence of the euro-dollar market.

Theory

In this section the portfolio theoretic approaches of, for example, Black [1971], Steib [1973] and Hewson and Sakakibara [1974] in the treatment of euro-dollar transactions is extended to embrace domestic monetary and international monetary transactions outside the euro-dollar market. (During the publication lag, Hewson and Sakakibara [1976] have produced a similar analysis.) Since our concern is with euro-dollars the world is divided into the U.S. and the rest of the world (ROW). Under these simplified circumstances four main international financial transactions may be identified:

A: net transactions between the U.S. and the euro-banks i.e. deposits minus liabilities.

B: gross transactions between the U.S. and ROW, i.e. U.S. deposits in ROW.

C: net transactions between ROW and the euro-banks,

i.e. deposits minus liabilities.

D: gross transactions between ROW and U.S. i.e. ROW's deposits in U.S.

B minus D will therefore equal the net transactions between the U.S. and ROW and A plus C will equal total transactions in stock terms of both the U.S. and ROW with the euro-dollar market. Since in equilibrium euro-dollar deposits must equal the assets of the euro-banks the euro-dollar market will clear when:

$$A + C = Q \qquad (9.1)$$

where Q is the net indebtedness, i.e. liabilities minus deposits of central monetary institutions with the euro-dollar market. Therefore, A and C denote net private positions.

We now examine the determinants of A, B, C and D from the point of view of portfolio theory. A is likely to vary directly with the differential between the euro-dollar rate (r_e) and U.S. interest rates (r_{us}). If this differential rises deposits would be switched from New York to the euro-banks and U.S. borrowing from the euro-banks would be curtailed in favour of domestic borrowing on the New York market. A is also likely to vary inversely with the differential between interest rates in ROW (r_w) and the euro-dollar rate, since the euro-banks and the banks in ROW are in competition for transactions with U.S. agents. Thus if the euro-dollar rate rises, *ceteris paribus*, U.S. agents switch deposits from both ROW and New York into the euro-dollar market. We may therefore write the determinants of A as:

$$A = a_1 (r_e - r_{us}) - a_2 (r_w - r_e) \qquad (9.2)$$

An analogous set of arguments applies to the determination of C. If the differential between the euro-dollar rate and domestic interest rates in ROW widens, agents in ROW would switch their deposits to the euro-banks from the banks in ROW. If, on the other hand New York rates rise relative to the euro-dollar rate agents in ROW would run down their net position with the euro-banks in favour of New York. We may therefore write the determinants of C as:-

$$C = c_1 (r_e - r_w) - c_2 (r_{us} - r_e) \qquad (9.3)$$

Equations 9.2 and 9.3 may be substituted into 9.1 to determine the euro-dollar rate in terms of r_{us} and r_w, e.g. Black [1971] and Steib [1973]. However, in principle r_{us} and r_w will not only be linked with the euro-dollar rate and through the euro-dollar market, but they will be linked by direct capital account transactions between the U.S. and ROW, i.e. B minus D.

B is likely to vary directly with the differential between r_w and r_{us} since U.S. agents' gross transactions with ROW would be greater if their deposits in ROW earn a higher return than in New York. However, B will also depend, as we have already seen, on the difference between r_w and r_e since to U.S. agents deposits in ROW are substitutes for euro-dollar deposits. The determinants of B may subsequently be written as:

$$B = b(r_w - r_{us}) + a_2(r_w - r_e) \tag{9.4}$$

D would be determined analogously to B. If U.S. rates rise, *ceteris paribus*, agents in ROW would switch their deposits from banks in ROW to New York and from the euro-banks to the New York banks. Hence we may write:

$$D = d(r_{us} - r_w) + c_2(r_{us} - r_e) \tag{9.5}$$

In practice, because euro-dollars and New York dollars are denominated in the same currency there will be no exchange risk to consider and c_2 is likely to be proportionately larger than d and c, i.e. dollar deposits are closer substitutes for each other than deposits of different currency denominations. Similarly, b and a, are likely to be proportionately larger than a_2.

We now turn to the determinants of domestic monetary transactions in the U.S. and ROW in the context of the international financial transactions that have been identified. The demand for money in the U.S. is hypothesised to vary inversely with domestic interest rates and domestic nominal income (Y_{us}):

$$M_{us}^d = -g_1 r_{us} + g_2 Y_{us} \tag{9.6}$$

Analogously, in ROW we have:

$$M_w^d = -e_1 r_w + e_2 Y_w \tag{9.7}$$

The supply of money in the U.S. is equal to the domestic credit that has been created in the U.S. (Z_{us}) less U.S. net indebtedness with the euro-banks and ROW since these constitute outflows from the U.S. domestic monetary system. We may therefore write the U.S. money supply as:

$$M_{us}^s = Z_{us} - A - B + D \tag{9.8}$$

Analogously the money supply in ROW would be:

$$M_w^s = Z_w + B - C - D \tag{9.9}$$

Thus the U.S. money supply would be **greater** than domestic credit created in the U.S. if the U.S. has been running capital account surpluses with ROW either directly or indirectly via the euro-dollar market. Under the circumstances the opposite would be true for ROW.

The system is closed by assuming that in equilibrium the demand and supplies for money are equated:

$$M^d{}_{us} = M^s{}_{us} \qquad \text{(i)}$$
$$M^d{}_w = M^s{}_w \qquad \qquad \text{(ii)} \qquad (9.10)$$

For simplicity we abstract from the determination of nominal incomes and the current account of the balance of payments and the exchange rate between dollars and the currency of ROW is implicitly assumed to be fixed. Our interest focuses on the potential determination of the interest rates via the set of possible capital account transactions.

Equations 9.1 and 9.10 determine r_e, r_{us} and r_w respectively. Substituting the remaining equations into these the following system is obtained:

$$\begin{bmatrix} \alpha_1 & -\alpha_2 & -\alpha_3 \\ -\alpha_2 & \beta_1 & -\beta_2 \\ -\alpha_3 & -\beta_2 & \beta_3 \end{bmatrix} \begin{bmatrix} r_e \\ r_{us} \\ r_w \end{bmatrix} = \begin{bmatrix} Q \\ g_2 Y_{us} - Z_{us} \\ e_2 Y_w - Z_w \end{bmatrix} \qquad (9.11)$$

where

$$\begin{aligned}
\alpha_1 &= a_1 + a_2 + c_1 + c_2 & \text{(i)} \\
\alpha_2 &= a_1 + c_2 & \text{(ii)} \\
\alpha_3 &= a_2 + c_1 & \text{(iii)} \\
\beta_1 &= a_1 + b + d + c_2 + g_1 & \text{(iv)} \\
\beta_2 &= b + d & \text{(v)} \\
\beta_3 &= b + a_2 + c_1 + d + e_1 & \text{(vi)}
\end{aligned} \qquad (9.12)$$

The determinant of the system is unambiguously positive:

$$det = \alpha_2(\beta_2 e_1 + \beta_3 g_1) + \alpha_3(\beta_2 g_1 + \beta_1 e_1) \qquad (9.13)$$

The solutions for the interest rates in terms of the exogenous variables are:

$$r_e = \frac{1}{det}\Big[(\beta_1\beta_3 - \beta_2{}^2)Q + (\alpha_2\beta_3 + \alpha_3\beta_2)(g_2 Y_{us} - Z_{us})$$
$$+ (\alpha_2\beta_2 + \alpha_3\beta_1)(e_2 Y_w - Z_w) \Big] \qquad \text{(i)}$$

$$r_{us} = \frac{1}{det}\Big[(\alpha_2\beta_3 + \alpha_3\beta_2)Q + (\alpha_1\beta_3 - \alpha_3{}^2)(g_2 Y_{us} - Z_{us}) \quad (9.14)$$
$$+ (\alpha_1\beta_2 + \alpha_2\alpha_3)(e_2 Y_w - Z_w) \Big] \qquad \text{(ii)}$$

$$r_w = \frac{1}{det}\Big[(\alpha_2\beta_2 + \alpha_3\beta_1)Q + (\alpha_1\beta_2 + \alpha_2\alpha_3)(g_2 Y_{us} - Z_{us})$$
$$+ (\alpha_1\beta_1 - \alpha_2{}^2)(e_2 Y_w - Z_w) \Big] \qquad \text{(iii)}$$

Equation 9.14i indicates that the euro-dollar rate is likely to vary directly with nominal incomes and inversely with domestic credit creation in the U.S. and ROW. When incomes rise domestic interest rates are increased, generating a contraction of euro-dollar deposits in favour of domestic deposits and an increase in desired euro-dollar borrowing. This net excess demand for euro-dollar borrowing is eliminated by a rise in the euro-dollar rate. The opposite effects occur when domestic credit (Z_w) is increased. Domestic monetary conditions ease pushing down domestic interest rates and an *ex ante* excess supply of euro-dollar deposits is generated. Noting that $\beta_1 \beta_3 > \beta_2{}^2$, equation 9.14i implies that net official borrowing on the euro-dollar market would put upward pressure on the euro-dollar rate.

As expected, equations 9.14 i − ii indicate that domestic interest rates vary directly with nominal incomes and the creation of domestic credit in the U.S. and ROW (noticing that $\alpha_1 \beta_3 > \alpha_3{}^2$ and that $\alpha_1 \beta_1 > \alpha_2{}^2$). However, it should be recalled for example that the final effect of an increase in Z_{us} on r_{us} occurs through a complex system of domestic and direct and indirect international financial portfolio adjustments. These equations further imply that official euro-dollar borrowing increases domestic interest rates via its effect on the euro-dollar rate itself.

Empirical Analysis

The objective in this section is to assess the relative influence on the euro-dollar rate of monetary factors in the U.S. and ROW in the light of the model described. One possibility would be that the euro-dollar rate is dominated by U.S. monetary factors because New York dollars and euro-dollars are likely to be such close substitutes relative to deposits of different currencies where exchange risk is likely to reduce the elasticity of substitution. On the other hand ROW is sizeable relative to the U.S. financial market and this could imply a high correlation between r_w and r_e.

Substituting from equation 9.3 and 9.4 into equation 9.1 and solving for the euro-dollar rate, we find that it is a weighted average of U.S. and world interest rates:

$$r_e = \frac{(a_1 + c_2)r_{us} + (a_2 + c_1)r_w + Q}{a_1 + c_2 + a_2 + c_1} \tag{9.15}$$

It also depends on official transactions in the euro-dollar market. If $a_1 + c_2$ is large relative to $a_2 + c_1$ U.S. interest rates will dominate the euro-dollar rate. However, these relative weights are essentially an empirical issue.

In practice, investors will have to choose whether or not to cover their euro-dollar operations in the forward market. The analysis so far has ignored this possibility since for simplicity the investor only had the uncovered option. In general, therefore, the euro-dollar rate would be a weighted average of the covered world interest rate, i.e. r_w minus the cost of forward cover against the dollar (*CFC*) and the uncovered world interest rate, which is r_w minus the expected rate of appreciation of the dollar (x). Thus, instead of equation 9.15 we have:

$$r_e = \frac{v_1 r_{us} + v_2 (r_w - CFC) + v_3 (r_w - x) + Q}{v_1 + v_2 + v_3} \qquad (9.16)$$

The euro-dollar rate is therefore expected to vary inversely with the expected rate of appreciation of the dollar and the cost of forward cover.

The expected rate of appreciation of the dollar given our observation period is hypothesised to depend on the ratio of U.S. official liabilities to gold reserves. Thus as this ratio widens world investors judge that the role of the U.S. as world banker is weakened and confidence in the dollar weakens. However, expectations may evolve over time, in which case we write:

$$x = \sum_i w_i \frac{G}{XLUS} t - i \qquad (9.17)$$

where G = U.S. gold reserves (source: *Business Conditions Digest*); *XLUS* = U.S. Official Liabilities to overseas (source: *Business Conditions Digest*).

Quarterly data were used for an estimation period 1960–72. The principal result was that the three-month euro-dollar deposit rate is if anything equally determined by monetary conditions outside the U.S. as inside the U.S. and that the three-month U.S. CD rate is not the most efficient predictor of the euro-dollar rate. Indeed, equation 9.18 where the CD rate is the sole explanatory variable has highly serially correlated errors.

$$r_e = 0.62219 \, r_{CD} + 3.2 \qquad (9.18)$$
$$(7.68)$$

$$R^2 = 0.53 \qquad 0 = 1.29 \qquad DW = 0.26$$

Interest rate data are averages of end-month observations. The sources are as follows:

Euro-dollar deposit rate and three-month U.K. local authority deposit rate: *Bank of England Quarterly Bulletin*. U.S. CD rate and prime commercial paper rate: *Federal Reserve Bulletin*.

Canadian Treasury Bill rate: *Bank of Canada Statistical Summary*.

Frankfurt three-month money market rate: *Deutscher Bundesbank Monthly Review*.

French three-month inter-bank rate: compiled by Bank of England.

There were no available data on Q.

Attempts to specify non-U.S. interest rates resulted in the coefficient on the CD rate becoming statistically insignificant. Indeed, U.S. rates were represented by the yield on prime commercial paper ($RPCP$), the interpretation of this being that as yields rise in the U.S. both the private and banking sectors wish to borrow in the euro-dollar market, thereby exerting upward pressure on the euro-dollar rate. This is shown by equation 9.19:

$$r_e = 0.54 + 0.46343\,RPCP + 0.66\,r^*_w - \sum_{i=1}^{7} w_i \frac{G}{XLUS} t - i \qquad (9.19)$$
$$\quad\quad\quad (3.31) \qquad\qquad (5.5)$$

$$w_i = 0.0005 \quad 0.00086 \quad 0.00107 \quad 0.001143 \quad 0.0010715$$
$$\quad (1.92) \quad\; (1.92) \quad\;\; (1.92) \quad\;\; (1.92) \quad\;\;\; (1.92)$$

$$0.000857 \quad 0.0005 \quad \Sigma = 0.006$$
$$(1.92) \quad\quad (1.92)$$

$$R^2 = 0.96 \quad \sigma = 0.385 \quad DW = 1.31$$

where r^*_w is a weighted average of non-U.S. covered interest rates, based on the Frankfurt three-month money market rate (0.15) the Canadian Treasury Bill rate (0.6), the French three-month inter-bank rate (0.05) and the U.K. three-month local authority deposit rate (0.2). These weights were derived by direct specification of these interest rates. This specification carried the degree of autocorrelation into the indeterminate zone and reduces the standard error of estimate very substantially. Unweighted estimates generated difficulties because of the high degree of collinearity between the non-U.S. covered interest rates. The weights were derived by specifying each non-U.S. rate on its own and then weighting together these estimated coefficients. Finally an F test confirmed that the weighted approach was superior to unweighted estimation.

The equation implies that world interest rates have had a greater effect on the euro-dollar rate than U.S. rates represented here by the rate of prime commercial paper. This could be justified in terms of the relative sizes of the monetary systems in the U.S. and the rest of the world. The sum of the coefficients on $RPCP$ and r^*_w is not significantly different from unity, i.e. in accordance with the theory that has been discussed. There is, however, a discrepancy between the specification in equation 9.19 and the specification in equation 9.16. Attempts to estimate equation 9.16 or to re-express the numerator as $v_1 r_{us} + (v_2 + v_3) r_w - v_2 CFC - v_3 x$ were not successful. The equation suggests that if for example the U.K. authorities attempt to raise domestic interest rates by say 1 per cent in order to widen the covered differential in its favour, there will be a 0.132 per cent offset in the euro-dollar market itself because of higher net euro-dollar borrowing. In the Canadian case this effect is even stronger. Equation 9.19 also shows that as the U.S. gold reserves ratio improves, confidence in the dollar strengthens and the additional demand for euro-dollar deposits that this brings about tends to soften euro-dollar rates. However, it would seem that this confidence effect was weak both in magnitude and statistical significance. The distributed lag estimates are based on a quadratic polynomial with initial and final weights constrained to pass through zero.

No success was achieved in identifying the influence of regulations D and M on the euro-dollar rate via New York borrowing. However, Steib [1973] reports some encouraging results in these respects. Occasionally the expected negative coefficient was obtained but since it was never significant it was dropped from the preferred equation 9.19. Similarly the interest equalisation tax and the voluntary credit restraint programme which should have deflected borrowing off the New York market to the euro-dollar market and bid up euro-dollar rates were not significant when represented by dummy variables.

Being *OLS* results the coefficient on r_w^* is if anything likely to be biased downwards; for a random shock to the euro-dollar rate would tend to lower the forward component of r_w^*. This view is supported by the results set out in Table 9.1, where r_w^* is assumed to be simultaneously determined alongside r_e. U.S. interest rates on the other hand are assumed to be determined independently of overseas monetary conditions. This specification recognises the importance of world monetary conditions in the domestic monetary sectors of the non-U.S. economies that are party to the model. Apart from the predetermined variables in the equations reported in the table, additional instrumental variables are U.S. *GDP* and export price competitiveness, *RPCP*, $G/XLUS$ and U.S. long-term bond yields. χ_1^2 tests the hypothesis that the instruments as a group are independent of the error term. $\chi_1^{2}*$ is the critical value of χ_1^2 at the 95 per cent level. Similarly, χ_2^2 tests the hypothesis that a sixth-order correlogram of estimated residuals is randomly distributed where $\chi_2^{2}*$ is the critical value. γ is the coefficient on a first-order autoregressive error process.

With the exception of the first three equations in Table 9.1, the coefficient of r_w^* is higher than its value in equation 9.19 and it is interesting to note that where in the sixth equation the specification of instruments was most satisfactory in terms of $\chi_1^{2}*$ the coefficient on r_w^* is the largest. However, in general it proved difficult to obtain a satisfactory specification of instruments at the 95 per cent level, although not under a more lax confidence limit.

Equation 5 suggests that when the CD rate is used a first-order partial

TABLE 9.1 Determinants of the Euro-dollar Deposit Rate *

				Equation				
	1	2	3	4	5	6	7	8
Constant	-0.16587 (0.9)	-.01446 (0.04)	-.18532 (0.52)	-0.8355 (1.82)	-0.69648 (2.2)	1.56246 (2.84)		-0.66883 (1.63)
$RPCP$	0.6823 (3.67)	1.03776 (5.11)	0.92381 (3.43)					0.3294 (1.45)
r_{CD}			-0.07326 (0.32)	0.50781 (3.19)	0.3105 (2.61)	0.00682 (0.05)	0.29722 (3.63)	
$r_{e_{t-1}}$					0.18627 (2.33)			
$(G/XLUS)_{t-1}$						-0.02093 (4.98)	-0.01055 (4.79)	-0.00767 (2.32)
r^*_w	0.51466 (2.69)	0.12436 (0.61)	0.33451 (2.03)	0.85229 (7.41)	0.79859 (7.26)	1.04109 (14.4)	0.97824 (13.4)	0.78372 (3.7)
χ^2_1 (χ^{2*}_1)	18.0 (14.1)	6.8 (12.6)	16.32 (14.1)	19.54 (14.1)	17.61 (15.5)	7.46 (16.9)	14.57 (16.9)	16.6 (15.5)
χ^2_2 (χ^{2*}_2)	16.66 (12.6)	11.25 (12.6)	9.63 (12.6)	4.4 (12.6)	4.36 (12.6)	9.9 (12.6)	3.41 (12.6)	8.38 (12.6)
γ		0.49186 (3.87)	0.51912 (3.46)					
σ	0.394	0.398	0.37	0.423	0.411	0.357	0.381	0.383

't' values in brackets.   * Estimation programme written by D. F. Hendry

adjustment process reduces the standard error of estimate. However, when *RPCP* was specified this specification was no longer necessary. Equation 4, 5 and 7 in Table 9.1 violate the restriction that the sum of the coefficients on r_w^* and the representative U.S. rates should not be significantly different from unity.

Table 9.2 summarises the results of a spate of recent empirical investigations in this area. The important feature of this table is, with the exception of Fratianni and Savona, the surprisingly low weight of U.S. rates in the determination of the euro-dollar rate. Both Tables 9.1 and 9.2 suggest that when *RPCP* is specified rather than the CD rate, the weight on U.S. rates rises. With the exception of Hewson and Sakakibara the general tenor of these studies is to confirm our own result that German rates are more important than U.K. rates in determining the euro-dollar rate. This result is not altogether surprising since the German monetary system is considerably larger than that of the U.K. Yet the equation with the lowest standard error and which best satisfied the simultaneity test – equation 6 in Table 9.1 – suggests the converse. However, we have already noted how in Chapter 7 U.K. capital flows are more interest-elastic than either West German or French capital flows in relation to the euro-dollar rate.

Conclusions

The theoretical model developed proved to be a useful empirical basis for analysing the proximate determinants of the euro-dollar deposit rate where the 'rest of the world' is conceived in terms of the U.K, Canada, France and Germany. On the whole the evidence suggests that the euro-dollar rate is not dominated by U.S. monetary conditions. Indeed, there is a growing consensus in the empirical literature to this effect.

It should be recalled from the discussion in Chapter 6, however, that an increase in r_w, i.e. the uncovered world interest rate, is unlikely to increase its covered counterpart by the same amount since part of the increase in r_w will be offset by movements in the cost of forward cover through the processes of covered-interest arbitrage. Accordingly, the euro-dollar rate would tend to be partially insulated from monetary developments in ROW. Equally, and for similar reasons, the relative role of New York rates would be enhanced since an increase in r_{us} would cause covered world interest rates to rise in sympathy via the covered interest arbitrage link in the forward market. Since covered transactions preclude exchange risk and since U.S. GDP constitutes about 35 per cent of world GDP we should expect that the coefficient of New York rates would be about 0.35. On the whole the reported results concur with this simplified view. But when the influence of New York and ROW rates on the cost of forward cover is taken into consideration, New York rates will tend to dominate the euro-dollar rate leaving only a marginal role for uncovered interest rates in ROW.

TABLE 9.2 Comparative Results

| | RPCP | Interest Rate | | | Switzerland | Germany | U.K. |
		USTB	U.S. Fed Funds	U.S. CD			
Marston [1974]	0.44	0.28			0.24	0.245*	0.26*
Black [1971]		0.77	0.35				0.1†
Fratianni and Savona [1972]	1.1						0.57
Hewson and Sakakibara [1974]		0.202	0.269			0.175*	0.3*
Rich [1972]		0.6	0.3				0.1
Steib [1973]				0.42		1.21*	0.36*
Argy and Hodjera [1973]		0.622				0.216	0.125

* Covered.
† Cost of forward cover only.

10 Overview and Conclusions

It has been the intention throughout this book to be as policy-oriented as possible, not only with regard to the empirical discussions but perhaps even more importantly with regard to the more theoretical sections. Indeed, it is arguable that an *a priori* approach to an appraisal of macro-economic policy has much to commend it in view of what might loosely be called 'the econometric problem'. In an ideal world where precisely formulated hypotheses can be tested fairly un-ambigously against an abundance of data that are readily available, scientific progress may proceed along the lines of 'conjectures and refutations' conceptualised by Popper [1963] and others. Social scien-tists, however, not only find it difficult to form precise hypotheses, but they are also invariably unable to perform controlled experiments and the data that are available are frequently inappropriate to the hy-potheses under consideration.

Economists are additionally confronted with 'the econometric prob-lem' which refers to the confounding nature of multicollinearity, serial correlation of the errors, simultaneous equations bias, unobservable variables, etc., which may often be crucial. Thus even when we have managed to formulate relatively crude hypotheses such as Y depends on X (and without limiting ourselves to the precise form of this function, both regarding statics and dynamics) we are most of the time never certain whether the data have corroborated or falsified a hypothesis, or whether 'the econometric problem' is creating difficulties. Often what happens is that a formulation is eventually found which has 'respectable' statistical properties. In these cases it is almost as if, in the spirit of 'seek and ye shall find', the hypotheses are accepted as fact and that the role of econometric investigation is to find some plausible empirical orders of magnitude and dynamic characteristics for a set of *a priori* pre-dispositions.

But even here 'the econometric problem' makes it difficult to distinguish between various estimates. Subsequently, there is more merit than usual in economists appraising macro-economic policy along *a priori* lines and there are more dangers than usual in economists adhering to the strict implications of their empirical estimates. The empirical estimates that have been reported in the preceding chapters are equally subject to these strictures. Clearly this does not imply that econometric research should be abandoned (otherwise why write this book?); we are bound to try to be as scientific as possible, but the limitations of econometric modelling must be accepted.

With these considerations in mind we tie together some of the diverse strands of thought that have appeared from time to time in this volume. We begin by considering the relationship between the two parts of the book.

Positive and Normative Economics

Table 7.3 summarised the likely responses of the capital accounts in a number of countries to various policy measures. The main conclusions were that forward intervention and policies towards long-term interest rates are likely to be more effective policy instruments regarding the balance of payments. Indeed forward intervention may be more effective and long-term interest rate policies as effective as the more traditional short-term money market policies. It should be clear from the context of this book that these conclusions were positive rather than normative. It is not being suggested that the authorities *should* in fact pursue more aggressive forward market policies or long-term interest rate policies, but that if they did they might enjoy a greater degree of leverage over the capital account. Nor does this reservation depend on the econometric humility that has been suggested in the preceding paragraphs.

Whether or not spot market intervention via the forward market or any other policy is desirable has already been discussed in Chapter 5, and it will be recalled that the substantive issue was whether or not expectations were formed rationally. Basically, if the authorities believe that when all issues of risk and uncertainty are taken into consideration the market has got the wrong set of prices, then aggregate welfare may be improved by activists or discretionary policy intervention. It should be recalled, however, that when the authorities do intervene they are not spending their own resources but those of the taxpayer, in which case it is possible that a proper evaluation of risk (i.e. the evaluation that the taxpayer himself would make) will not be made.

If the conditions for an activist set of policies are fulfilled, the next question is what is the most efficient combination of discretionary policies in the various markets? To answer this question it is not only necessary to know the welfare effects of the macro-economy in disequilibrium, but also the macro-economic impact of all the various policy measures. Armed with this information it is meaningful to perform optimal control calculations of macro-economic strategy. In this context the estimates reported in Chapters 6 and 7 would be relevant since they explore the relationship between a number of policy instruments and a number of macro-economic aggregates.

Expectations

The corroboration of the rational expectations hypothesis has been postulated in Chapter 4 to be the *sine qua non* of non-discretionary macro-economic policies. As it were, if the market has got its prices right the authorities by definition cannot act to improve matters. Table 7.2 indicates that at least as far as the foreign exchange market is concerned the data are consistent with the hypothesis that investors try to forecast the future in a rational way. Other researchers have reported consistency in their areas e.g. Sargent [1973] regarding inflationary expectations, Modigliani and Shiller [1973] regarding interest rates and McCallum [1975] regarding the labour market. The 'econometric problem' most probably implies that the data could be shown to be consistent with other hypotheses about the formation of expectations and in this study this exercise or test has not been attempted. However, it would have been a cause for concern if the data had not been consistent with the rational expectations hypothesis, instead of a cause for rejoicing that they were.

Since so much depends on the rational expectations hypothesis and since it is likely to be difficult to find hard enough evidence either to accept or reject it, how might the dilemma be resolved? Most probably intuition will serve as the best arbiter. Just as it seems reasonable to assume that all men are innocent until proven guilty, it seems reasonable to believe that all men are rational unless there are obvious signs to the contrary. After all, the rational expectations hypothesis merely asserts that people will construct the best possible view of the future that they can in the light of the information that is at their disposal. Indeed, since resources and money are at stake it would be difficult to understand why they should seek to behave otherwise, short of speculative masochism. The opponents of the rational expectations hypothesis are effectively saying that people do not act in their own best interests and that the authorities are better equipped to look after the interests of the people than the people themselves. This may be so, but intuitively it seems unlikely; one could even argue that it is a form of authoritarian cynicism.

Subsequently, there is an axiomatic case to be made for the rational expectations hypothesis which has an analogous relationship with the maximisation principle in economics. Just in the same way as it seems reasonable to accept that people will act in a way which to them is most efficient—the maximisation principle—it seems reasonable to accept that people will take the best possible view of the future—the rationality principle. To reject either of these intuitive principles would only be justified on the strongest of empirical grounds. It follows from this that the rationality principle should be accepted as a matter of course until there are clear reasons for rejecting it.

The Appropriate Model

Each econometrician will unearth a different model from the data but most probably many will be working on the basis of the same intellectual structure. Indeed, the intellectual ingredients described in Chapter 2 are most probably acceptable to the majority of model builders today. Indeed, they were collated from actual models and are not original. Likewise, the estimates in Part B may not be repeated by others (although the results reviewed suggest a gathering empirical consensus on certain issues) but the logical framework is most probably generally acceptable.

If the axioms of the consensus model summarised in Chapter 2 are rejected then the logical deductions described in Chapter 3 would no longer obtain. For example, if the stock-flow logic of the monetary theory is rejected or if the concept of the market is abandoned, the deductions in Chapter 3 would be false. Whether to accept or reject this model as being appropriate is a matter of taste. However, if the model is accepted, this is more important than its empirical flesh and blood since the policy implications are unlikely to depend so crucially on them in the context that has been set.

Consequently the appropriate model does not depend on whether the marginal propensity to import is 0.3, or the income elasticity of the demand for money is 0.7, etc.; but whether these propensities and elasticities are accepted in the first place. However, it should be recalled from Chapter 3 that the long-run properties of the model may be sensitive to its dynamic characteristics as well as its technical structure regarding non-linearity, etc.

Implementing Policy Rules

In the wake of the 'Keynesian Revolution' the challenge was to discover the best way of formulating discretionary policies. In many respects these have been good and even exciting times for civil servants, officials and policy makers whose role it was to be active and on the alert. In contrast, the non-discretionary policy philosophy that is implied by much of the argumentation in this book may appear to lack much of the charm and glamour of its precursor. It is therefore understandable that difficulties may arise in disestablishing the activist school of policy.

However, the implementation of rules has its own challenges (apart from patience) and it would be misleading to assume that the professional expertise, acumen and activism required by such a policy strategy is any less formidable than that required by the activist policy philosophy. It is merely that the focus of this expertise, acumen and activism is different.

For example, if some form of a monetary rule were accepted such as that the money supply should grow by 3 per cent per annum, does this mean that the annual rate of growth should be adhered to on a weekly, monthly and quarterly basis too? Also, given the lags in the collection of money supply data the money supply may be off target without the authorities knowing about it. Therefore, are there any lead indicators to which the authorities might refer to avoid the dangers of instrument instability in the pursuit of their money growth target? Furthermore, what constitutes a significant deviation from the target? Presumably, the authorities would not envisage that their task was to maintain a 100 per cent record with respect to the target since there will inevitably be the random factors causing day-to-day deviations which would not constitute a significant aberration from the target.

Even when these issues have been settled it remains to consider the open-market policies required to implement the monetary rule. In this context, what is the appropriate balance between long and short-term open market policies? In other words, the philosophy of policy passivity has its own genre of professional activism; it is only its focus that is different.

Micro-economic Policies

As pointed out in Chapter 4 the speed of adjustment of the model that was discussed depended on a variety of parameters. If a policy of macro-economic passivism is required, the only conceivable way in which disequilibria may be reduced is at the micro-economic level of seeking to alter these parameters. For example if labour is more mobile there would be less of a tendency for disequilibria to persist. In this context, a greater degree of competition in the labour markets would be desirable too since any predispositions about appropriate wage rates or labour force sizes would serve to slow down the *tâtonnement* process. The same applies to restrictions and monopolistic practices in the financial and goods markets. Fixed interest rates and prices are almost bound to protract the adjustment process towards equilibrium since the degrees of freedom are less.

All these and related considerations belong in the micro rather than the macro-economic domain, yet they could make an important contribution to the more efficient operation of the macro-economy as a whole. In many cases, however, the sluggish responses of the macro-

economy are due directly or indirectly to the previous policies of the
authorities in the various markets such as housing, labour, finance, etc.

Political Economy

During the last few years in particular a number of domestic economies
and the world economy have shown signs of strain. Many countries have
experienced high rates of inflation at the same time as unemployment
has been high and balance of payments deficits have been soaring.
During the 1960s prices and incomes policies began to be more widely
used as a means for controlling inflation and this development has
extended into the 1970s.

No attempt will be made here to assess whether in fact prices and
incomes policies achieved any lasting benefits. Instead we focus on the
strategic implications of these policies in the light of the policy
philosophy hitherto discussed. Prices and incomes policies are features
of what might loosely be called the 'controlled economy'. In the
'controlled economy' the principal economic aggregates are determined
by direct control or edict. Prices and incomes policies would serve to
control prices and wages. The balance of payments would be controlled
by import and capital controls and economic growth would be
controlled by the authorities who in a mixed economy would invest
when the private sector had refrained. The 'controlled economy' would
be supported by a structure of taxes and subsidies and most probably
since prices would be controlled some form of rationing would be
required. Likewise with the labour market.

While many governments have experimented with wages and price
controls they have baulked at serious balance of payments controls in
face of international pressures. However, the political pressures for the
state to invest where the private sector has not done so are strong in a
number of industrial countries and have manifested themselves for some
time.

Political economy in a number of industrial countries has been at an
important cross-roads for some time. Originally the hope had been that
the policy assignment philosophy of Tinbergen, Mundell and others
would enable the authorities to select their economic objectives and to
achieve them with the available policy tools. However, this has not been
particularly successful and as pointed out in Chapter 5 is not logically
feasible in the long term. One interpretation of events would be that the
long term has arrived in a number of industrial countries.

If so, the choices are fundamentally two-fold. One possibility is to
embrace the 'controlled economy' in its entirety because most probably
it will be difficult to control one part of the economy without controlling
the other. The other possibility is to abandon the principles of policy

activism and to give the economy a chance to find its own level and to learn to come to terms with itself. This form of political economy would concentrate on micro-economic improvements while macro-economic policy would be based on some form of policy rule. In their own way, most probably either of these two systems would work and the centrally-planned countries have had much experience with the 'controlled economy'. Many would doubt whether the *via media* of the 'mixed-economy' is a long-run stable alternative between these two poles and some would claim that it has been responsible for bringing political economy to this cross-roads in the first place. Ultimately social and economic choice is political. Hopefully one of the contributions of this book has been to explore some of the implications of taking the alternative to the 'controlled economy'.

Bibliography

Adams, F. G., H. Eguchi and F. Meyer-zu-Schlochtern [1969], 'An Econometric Analysis of International Trade', *OECD Occasional Papers*, Paris.

Almon, S. [1965], 'The Distributed Lag Between Capital Appropriations and Expenditures', *Econometrica*, 33 (January).

Antier, D. [1973], 'Recherche d'une Schématization des Mouvements Internationaux des Capitaux à Court Terme', *Statistiques et Etudes Financières* No. 12: Ministère de l'Economie et des Finances, Paris.

Argy, V., and Z. Hodjera [1973], 'Financial Integration and Interest Rate Linkages in Industrial Countries', *IMF Staff Papers*, 20 (March).

Argy, V., and M. G. Porter [1972], 'The Forward Exchange Market and the Effects of Domestic and External Disturbances under Alternative Exchange Rate Systems', *IMF Staff Papers*, 19 (November).

Armington, p. [1969], 'A Theory of Demand for Products Distinguished by Place of Production', *IMF Staff Papers*, 16 (March).

Ball, R. J., T. Burns and J. S. E. Laury [1977], 'The Role of Exchange Rate Changes in Balance of Payments Adjustment; the United Kingdom Case', *Economic Journal*, 87 (March).

Barro, R. J. [1976], 'Rational Expectations and the Role of Monetary Policy', *Journal of Monetary Economics*, 2 (January).

Basevi, G. [1973], 'A Model for the Analysis of Official Intervention in the Foreign Exchange Markets', Chapter 7 in *International Trade and Money*, M. B. Connally and A. K. Swoboda (eds): Allen & Unwin, London.

Beenstock, M. [1976], 'Forward Exchange Markets, International Capital Movements and the Balance of Payments', Ph.D. dissertation: University of London.

Beenstock, M., and P. Minford [1976], 'A Quarterly Econometric Model of World Trade and Prices, 1955-1971', Chapters 5 in *Inflation in Open Economies*', M. Parkin and G. Zis (eds): Manchester University Press and University of Toronto Press.

Bell, G. [1973], *The Euro-dollar Market and the International Financial System*: Macmillan, London.

Black, S. W. [1971], 'An Econometric Study of Euro-dollar Borrowing by New York Banks and the Rate of Interest on Euro-dollars', *Journal of Finance*, 26 (March).

Black, S. W. [1973], 'International Money Markets and Flexible Exchange Rates', *Princeton Studies in International Finance*, No. 32: Princeton University Press, Princeton, N. J.

Boatwright, B. D., and G. A. Renton [1975], 'An Analysis of United Kingdom Inflows and Outflows of Direct Foreign Investment', *Review of Economics and Statistics*, 57 (November).

Branson, W. H. [1968], *Financial Capital Flows in the U.S. Balance of Payments*: North Holland Publishing Company, Amsterdam.

Branson, W. H. and R. D. Hill [1971], *Capital Movements in the OECD Area*: OECD, Paris.

Britton, A. J. C. [1970], 'The Dynamic Stability of the Foreign Exchange Market', *Economic Journal*, 80 (March).

Brunner, K. [1973], 'Money Supply Process and Monetary Policy in a Open Economy', Chapter 8 in *International Trade and Money*, M. B. Connally and A. K. Swoboda (eds): Allen & Unwin London.

Clendenning, E. W. [1970], *The Euro-dollar Market*: Oxford, Clarendon Press.

Clower, R. W. [1969], 'What Neoclassical Monetary Theory Really Wasn't', *Canadian Journal of Economics and Political Science*, 2 (May).

Cootner, P. H. (ed.) [1964], *The Random Character of Stock Market Prices*: MIT Press, Cambridge, Mass.

Cripps, F., and W. Godley [1976], 'A Formal Analysis of the Cambridge Economic Policy Group's Model', *Economica*, 43 (November).

Dornbusch, R. [1973], 'Currency Depreciation, Hoarding and Relative Prices', *Journal of Political Economy*, 81 (July/August).

Dornbusch, R. [1973], 'Revaluation, Money and Non-traded Goods', *American Economic Review*, 63 (December)

Fama, E. F. [1970], 'Efficient Capital Markets: A Review of Theory and Empirical Work', *Journal of Finance*, 25 (May).

Fetherstone, M. J. [1976], 'Technical Manual on the Cambridge Economic Policy Group Model', mimeo, Department of Applied Economics, Cambridge.

Fratianni, M., and P. Savona [1972], 'International Liquidity: An Analytical and Empirical Re-interpretation', Chapter 2 in *A Debate on the Euro-dollar Market*: *Quaderni di Ricerche*, No. 2.

Frenkel, J., and H. G. Johnson (eds) [1976], '*The Monetary Approach to the Balance of Payments*' : Allen & Unwin, London.

Frenkel, J. A., and R. M. Levitch [1975], 'Covered Interest Arbitrage: Unexploited Profits?', *Journal of Political Economy*, 83 (April)

Friedman, M. [1959], *A Program for Monetary Stability*: New York, Fordham University Press.

Friedman, M. [1968], 'The Role of Monetary Policy', *American Economic Review*, 58 (March)

Friedman, M. [1969], 'The Optimum Quantity of Money', Chapter 1 in *The Optimum Quantity of Money and Other Essays:* Chicago, Aldine Publishing Company.

Grubel, H. G. [1968], 'Forward Exchange, Speculation and the International Flow of Capital': Stanford University Press, Stanford, California.

Hahn, F. H. [1971], 'Professor Friedman's Views on Money', *Economica*, 38 (February).

Helliwell, J. F. [1969], 'A Structural Model of the Foreign Exchange Market', *Canadian Journal of Economics and Political Science*, 35 (February).

Helliwell, J. F., *et al.* [1971], *The Structure of RDX2*, Bank of Canada.

H. M. Treasury [1975], *Technical Manual,*: H. M. S. O., London.

Hester, D., and J. Tobin (eds) [1967], *Financial Markets and Economic Activity*: New York, John Wiley.

Hewson J., and E. Sakakibara [1974], 'The Euro-dollar Deposit Multiplier: A Portfolio Approach', *IMF Staff Papers*, 21 (July).

Hewson, J., and E. Sakakibara [1976], 'A General Equilibrium Approach to the Eurodollar Market', *Journal of Money Credit and Banking*, 8 (August).

Hodjera, Z. [1971], 'Short-term Capital Movements of the United Kingdom', *Journal of Political Economy*, 79 (July/August).

Hodjera, Z. [1973], 'International Short-term Capital Movements: A Survey of Theory and Empirical Analysis', *IMF Staff Papers*, 20 (November).

Hutton, J. P. [1977], 'A Model of Short-term Capital Movements, the Foreign Exchange Market and Official Intervention in the United Kingdom, 1963-70', *Review of Economic Studies*, 44 (February).

Hutton, J. P., and A. P. L. Minford [1975], 'A Model of U.K. Manufactured Exports and Export Prices', *Government Economic Service Occasional Papers*, No. 11, H.M.S.O., London.

Jasay, A. E. [1958], 'Bank Rate and Forward Exchange Rate Policy', *Banca Nazionale del Lavoro Quarterly Review*, 12 (March).

Johnson, H. G. [1958], 'Optimum Tariffs and Retaliation', Chapter 2 in *International Trade and Economic Growth*: Allen & Unwin, London.

Johnson, H. G. [1958], 'Towards a General Theory of the Balance of Payments', in *International Trade and Economic Growth*: Allen & Unwin, London.

Johnson, H. G. [1972], 'The Monetary Approach to Balance of Payments Theory', Chapter 11 in *International Trade and Money*, M. B. Connolly and A. K. Swoboda (eds): Allen & Unwin, London.

Johnson, H. G. [1976], 'The Monetary Theory of the Balance of Payments', Chapter 6 in *The Monetary Approach to the Balance of*

Payments, J. A. Frenkel and H. G. Johnson (eds): Allen & Unwin, London.

Kahn, R., and M. V. Posner [1974], 'Cambridge Economics and the Balance of Payments', *The Times*, London, 17-18. April.

Kesselman, J. [1971], 'The Role of Speculation in Forward Rate Determination: The Canadian Flexible Dollar, 1953-60', *Canadian Journal of Economics and Political Science*, 37 (August).

Keynes, J. M. [1923], *A Tract on Monetary Reform*: Macmillan, London.

Kouri, J. K., and M. G. Porter [1974], 'International Capital Flows and Portfolio Equilibrium', *Journal of Political Economy*, 82 (May/June).

Kydland, F. E., and E. C. Prescott [1977], 'Rules Rather than Discretion: The Inconsistency of Optimal Plans', *Journal of Political Economy*, 85 (June).

Labys, W. C., and C. W. J. Granger [1970], '*Speculation, Hedging and Commodity Price Forecasts*': Heath Lexington Books, Lexington, Mass.

Laidler, D. E. W. [1969], *The Demand for Money: Theories and Evidence*: International Textbook Company, Scranton, Pa.

Laidler, D. E. W. [1976], 'Expectations and the Phillips Trade-off: A Commentary', *Scottish Journal of Political Economy*, 23 (February).

Livesey, D. A. [1971], 'Optimising Short-term Economic Policy', *Economic Journal*, 81 (September).

Lucas, R. E. [1972], 'Expectations and the Neutrality of Money', *Journal of Economic Theory*, 4 (April)

Lucas, R. E. [1976], 'Econometric Policy Evaluation: A Critique', *Journal of Monetary Economics*, 1 (Supplement).

Marston, R. C. [1974], 'American Monetary Policy and the Structure of the Euro-dollar Market', *Princeton Studies in International Finance*, No. 34: Princeton University Press, Princeton, N. J.

McCallum, B. T. [1975], 'Rational Expectations and the Natural Rate Hypothesis: Some Evidence for the United Kingdom', *Manchester School*, 43 (March).

McCallum, B. T. [1977], 'The Role of Speculation in the Canadian Forward Exchange Market: Some Estimates using Rational Expectations', *Review of Economics and Statistics*, 59 (May).

Miller, M. H. [1973], 'Competition and Credit Control and the Open Economy', *Manchester School*, 41 (March).

Minford, A. P. L. [1975], 'Substitution Effects, Speculation and Exchange Rate Stability', mimeo, Manchester University.

Modigliani, F. [1977], 'The Monetarist Controversy or, Should we Forsake Stabilization Policies?', *American Economic Review*, 67 (March).

Modigliani, F., and R. J. Shiller [1973], 'Inflation, Rational Expectations and the Term Structure of Interest Rates', *Economica*, 40 (February).

Modigliani, F., and R. Sutch [1966], 'Innovations in Interest Rate Policy', *American Economic Review*, 56 (May).

Mundell, R. A. [1962], 'The Appropriate Use of Monetary and Fiscal Policy for Internal and external Stability', *IMF Staff Papers*, 9 (March).

Mundell, R. A. [1963], 'Capital Mobility and Stabilization Policies: Fixed and Flexible Exchange Rates', *Canadian Journal of Economics and Political Science*, 29 (November).

Muth, J. F. [1960], 'Optimal Properties of Exponentially Weighted Forecasts', *Journal of the American Statistical Association*, 55 (June).

Muth, J. F. [1961], 'Rational Expectations and the Theory of Price Movements', *Econometrica*, 29 (July).

Nerlove, M. [1958], 'Adaptive Expectations and Cobweb Phenomena', *Quarterly Journal of Economics*, 72 (May).

Officer, L. H., and T. D. Willet [1970], 'The Covered Arbitrage Schedule: A Critical Study of Recent Developments', *Journal of Money Credit and Banking*, 2 (May).

Phelps, E. S. (ed.) [1970], *Microfoundations of Employment and Inflation Theory*: Norton, New York.

Pindyck, R. S. [1973], *Optimal Planning for Economic Stabilization; the Application of Control Theory to Stabilization Policy*,: North Holland Publishing Company, Amsterdam.

Pitchford, J. D., and Turnovsky S. J. (eds) [1977], *Applications of Control Theory to Economic Analysis*:   North Holland Publishing Company, Amsterdam.

Poole, W. [1976], 'Rational Expectations in the Macro Model', *Brookings Papers on Economic Activity*, No. 2.

Popper, K. R. [1963], 'Science: Conjectures and Refutations', Chapter 1 in *Conjectures and Refutations*: Routledge & Kegan Paul, London.

Porter, M. G. [1971], 'A Theoretical and Empirical Framework for Analyzing the Term Structure of Exchange Rate Expectations', *IMF Staff Papers*, 18 (November).

Porter, M. G. [1972], 'Capital Flows as an Offset to Monetary Policy: the German Experience', *IMF Staff Papers*, 19 (July).

Price, L. D. D. [1972], 'The Demand for Money in the U.K.: A Further Investigation', *Bank of England Quarterly Bulletin* (March).

Rich, G. [1972], 'A Theoretical and Empirical Analysis of the Euro-dollar Market', *Journal of Money Credit and Banking*, 4 (August).

Samuelson, L. [1974], 'A Model of International Trade', *OECD Occasional Papers*, Paris.

Samuelson, P. A. [1965], 'Proof that Properly Anticipated Prices Fluctuate Randomly'(*Sloane Management Review* (spring).

Sargent, T. J. [1973], 'Rational Expectations, the Real Rate of Interest and the Natural Rate of Unemployment', *Brookings Papers on Economic Activity*, No. 2

Sargent, T. J., and N. Wallace [1975], ' "Rational" Expectations, the Optimal Monetary Instrument and the Optimal Money Supply Rate', *Journal of Political Economy*, 83 (April).

Siegal, J. R. [1972], 'Risk, Interest and Forward Exchange', *Quarterly Journal of Economics*, 86.

Sohmen, E. [1966], 'The Theory of Forward Exchange', *Princeton Studies in International Finance*, No. 17: Princeton University Press, Princeton, N. J.

Spraos, J. [1972], 'The Arbitrage Function', Chapter 2 in *Le Change à Terme*, P. Coulbois (ed.): Editions Cujas, Paris.

Steib, S. B. [1973], 'The Demand for Euro-dollar Borrowing by U.S. Banks', *Journal of Finance*, 28 (September).

Stein, J. [1965], 'The Forward Rate and Interest Parity', *Review of Economic Studies*, 32 (April).

Stoll, H. B. [1968], 'An Empirical Study of the Forward Exchange Market under Fixed and Flexible Exchange Rate Systems', *Canadian Journal of Economics and Political Science*, 34 (February).

Telser, L. G. [1967], 'A Critique of Some Recent Empirical Work on the Explanation of the Term Structure of Interest Rates', *Journal of Political Economy*, 75 (August).

Tinbergen, J. [1956], *Economic Policy: Principles and Design*: North Holland Publishing Company, Amsterdam.

Tsiang, S. C. [1959], 'The Theory of Forward Exchange and the Effects of Government Intervention in the Forward Exchange Market', *IMF Staff Papers*, 6 (April)

Walters, A. A. [1971], 'Consistent Expectations, Lags and the Quantity Theory', *Economic Journal*, 81 (June).

Index